How Did My *Gardens* Grow?

Putting Life Puzzles Together for Better

BRENDA G. ELLER

To
my younger self,
everyone who shared this journey with me,
and anyone who sees themselves between the lines.

Contents

Foreword

You sow. You reap. You cut back, trim, and prune. You dig up and start over. You make a plan, but things that are out of your control attack, like deer in the dark. Sometimes it's beautiful, and sometimes it's dirty and ugly. Sound like your garden—or your life maybe? Ecclesiastes tells us there is a time and purpose for everything. As we walk in the flesh, that's often a hard pill to swallow. Especially the "purpose" part. Yet those of us who are strong Christ believers adhere to the belief that there is an ordained purpose and that good will prevail as we trust God to lead our way. It is what grounds us when things go awry.

It was through church that I first met Brenda, her husband Gary, and her daughter Kristyn some twenty years ago. I was a Sunday-morning greeter, and that's the way the friendship started. Brenda and I both had teenagers, and Lord knows we all need support raising teenagers! My background is in counseling, and I have worked extensively with teens and parents. As the current owner of a life-coaching practice for women, I work with many women who deal with relationship issues. Because it was a natural fit for me, I formed a support group for parents of teenagers to navigate teen/parent struggles. (We all know the list.) Brenda and Gary joined the support group, and it wasn't long before a bond had formed through confidential conversations between her and me. Trust evolved. At times, we rolled our eyes as we talked through the sheer absurdity of "teenagerness" until absurdity became pain. We muddled on through tears, frequently holding on to the prayers that were offered up to each other.

Feeling confused and alone, Brenda searched. She was passionate about her family and about her faith, although much of the time she felt alone, as do so many parents when faced with unfathomable circumstances. She crawled her way through her confusion, hoping to force change and come out on the other end. She questioned herself as a parent. Don't we all at some point?

It was not just being a parent of a teenager that brought about her trials. It was also the everyday ups and downs of life. Sometimes we walk through valleys that are so dark we can't see our way, kind of like being on a country road at midnight with no lights and no map. That's where she found herself during her darkest times as a single girl, a wife, and a mom—and it was dark. It was dark, it was getting late, and there was no map. All she had was the promise from God that He would take care while she remained steadfast in her faith. As a distraction, Brenda busied herself with projects, one after another. A lot of projects. Brenda is a mender. She is a builder, and she is a doer. With relationships or with things, she navigates the broken. Grass (pun intended) doesn't grow under her feet for long. Whether repositioning stonework or rebuilding a master plan, putting back together a broken doll, finding a use for a feather in a cabin, or completing a puzzle with a piece that's been missing for eons, she makes it all come together. She is determined. That's the mark of a person passionate about making things whole again and again, including herself. In reading this book, you will discover how each of those simple acts became an important part of Brenda's story.

As you will discover when reading, Brenda searched for the purpose of her trials. She told me years ago she was going to write a book about getting through her struggles, and I knew, if anyone had a story to tell, she did. She would write, work on it, and put it down according to her frame of mind and reference at the time. I was always anxious to see the final outcome, but, you know—when? Years passed. Books take a long time to come together. And how's she going to make this into a story? In the end, she did. She has written about some very private and painful times she lived through before she married, her journey of marriage itself and the struggles within, and of course parenting three children.

The thing that struck me most when reading was her authenticity, her rawness. It is rare to find someone as open and vulnerable as she has been in writing this book. Everyone has a story, but few are willing to be so vulnerable. That's exactly how the book pulled me in. No doubt, it will do the same for others, offering encouragement and inspiring many who are on their own quests. There is hope!

We have all the seasons in our gardens, just as Ecclesiastes tells us. How lovely it would be to have a "spring" life year-round, but we know we have those winters—those dark, dreary, overcast parts of our journeys. We have dismal seasons when everything—and sometimes everyone—seems dead to us just as the world outside does when we look out the kitchen window in mid-January and see nothing but drab. And so the analogy of life and a garden—well, it just works. To everything, there really is a season.

I am honored to write this foreword for Brenda, and I know, as readers move through this book, they will find themselves between the lines, weaving in and out of the pages. All of us have to learn to navigate the journeys on which we find ourselves, and in this book, Brenda shares her struggles and gives great insight into how to make it through without even a flashlight. No map. Just reality. Just perseverance. You stumble on rocks, but you get up, and you make it beautiful. She did.

—Shirley Meek Williams, MEd, CCLC

Introduction

2/6/2021

Pen and pad became the ground
To sow and grow my thoughts.
I'm glad I learned to read and write
So lessons could be taught.

Words of value and importance
Could not be ignored.
For decades, they'd been building up.
They've poured out my heart's door.

It's been twelve years and eight months since the idea for this book was conceived. Writing a book was *not* my idea and, at the time, wasn't on my bucket list. However, the book idea grew on me after I realized the "therapy" was working and would have lasting benefits that could outlive me. My writing garden was a place of retreat, a place where seeds of understanding were planted and grew. I began to write not as a way of creating a book but as a way to sort out my feelings. Sifting through my feelings as they became visible was a holistic approach to a complicated process. I thrived on the gift of being physically able to hold a pen and having a blank canvas on which to plant and paint the words.

Sowing seeds of self-care gave me a sense of control over uncontrollable things. Writing became a validating and healthy dumping ground. Words piled up, and each sheet of paper was placed in an antique maple wood chest of drawers. The practice of writing allowed me the freedom to express myself in authentic, vulnerable, and revealing ways that taught me new truths about myself. Paper and ink don't judge; one receives as the other freely gives. Eventually, I could *see* how I really felt (and had felt in the past) as emotion-packed words poured out of me, sometimes faster than I could write. Tangible evidence of what had been awaiting discovery turned into mounds of paper containing words, thoughts, and feelings that needed to be processed. That key information was necessary to help me understand who I was.

Pens, scrap paper, envelopes, paper towels, napkins, notepads, and any other form of nearby paper were put to good use. During this process of reflection and development, I came to a place of deeper understanding. True friends walked along beside me and helped me talk things out in compassionate and nonjudgmental ways. Casual acquaintances and complete strangers were in their God-orchestrated places to validate and confirm that I was on a great path toward healing and could help many people as I shared my life story. There were those who opened up to me about things even their family and closest friends do not know. My lips are sealed, and I appreciate their trust and confidence in me to keep their secret(s) safe.

I connected with countless sage thinkers and writers through books, articles, and blogs. Even though the authors and I may never meet, I related to them based on similar experiences. In 2014, an important book came out (©Danielle Bernock, *Emerging With Wings: A True Story of Lies, Pain, And The LOVE that Heals*, 4F Media, 2nd ed.). Danielle's profound words resonate with many, including me: "Trauma is personal. It does not disappear if it is not validated. When it is ignored or invalidated the silent screams continue internally heard only by the one held captive. When someone enters the pain and hears the screams healing can begin."

Any individual who chooses the counseling pathway, receiving personalized help from trained professionals, is a hero in my book. It was easier for me to share feelings, deep emotions, raw realities, and innermost thoughts in written form. Thus, I was able to avoid choking on audible words and becoming strangled by pain-filled thoughts as I made my way through this cathartic journey.

Private sessions with the "Wonderful Counselor, Mighty God, Everlasting Father, Prince of Peace" (Isaiah 9:6) worked out well for me. Prayer and writing helped me stay on track. Many of the words were for my eyes only and were later shredded. Other words, worthy of sharing, were gathered and carefully transplanted so they could grow and bloom in due time.

Writing helped me remember more vividly, and be honest with myself, about what really happened in each significant life scene. I slowly grew on the inside and became able to see those scenes for what they truly were as I watched the replays in my mind.

Enlightenment is a huge blessing in the unique adventure called *life*. God didn't allow any raw, ugly, or vital experience to be wasted in my life. Instead, He caused everything, even the crummiest crumbs, to turn into nourishing food for the soul. I am grateful for healing promises throughout Scripture. Psalm 147:3 comforts and soothes: "He heals the brokenhearted and binds up their wounds." Patiently, tenderly, and lovingly, He was mending my broken heart, and emotional wounds were being touched and healed.

In any journey to wholeness and peace, there are countless blessings worth acknowledging and sharing. Raw, cathartic writing enables the writer to be a surgeon of the soul.

GROWING PAINS

Each life is like a garden;
The seeds are all unique.
Heartaches and pain make each one grow
From depths no soul can reach.

Dark days will surely find us
Fertilized with rain and sun.
Stresses and strains will test and stretch;
Out of the dust, we'll run.

Wisdom is gained while living life,
Reaching new heights to fly.
Each undertaking creates risk—
Does one now dare to try?

Accepting life's tough challenges
Helps growth to stay on track.
Stay focused on God's radiant Light;
We grow most when cut back.

Brenda Eller
6/10/2009

Preface

Four words, *this too shall pass,* were difficult to believe and accept when unrelenting storms continued for three decades. Most of the storms came from people—different ones at different times—but the unresolved pain in the unprocessed mess lingered and worsened.

As a toddler, our youngest daughter, Kristyn, enjoyed drinking out of her special sippy cup because it never tipped over. Our grandchildren asked to use it through the years because they enjoyed feeling like a little kid again. I witnessed the joy it brought as they played with the cup trying to make it tip over. It always bounced back, standing upright after being pushed around. That little sippy cup is a fine example of how it is when God protects and cares for His children through the storms of life. Taking the hits was hard. However, I can look back over it all and know that God was providing. He was with us and gave our family the grace, strength, and protection we needed so we wouldn't fall over completely and choose to give up.

As I ponder how I could have responded to difficult people God saw fit to bring into my life, the only action that comes to mind is to have *melted 'em with mercy.* Kindness is a merciful action. Merciful actions are forgiving, compassionate, and gracious. These can be the most difficult gifts to give another when we are hurting, yet kindness given through love is what we long to receive ourselves. Instead of stepping on dreams and crushing spirits, kindness is a salve that reaches, gently touches, and helps soothe the deepest of wounds. Sharing kindness through love is a way of giving comfort to pain-ridden souls. It helps the receiver and blesses the giver. Acts of kindness create win-win situations.

Our family was forced to grow in wisdom, knowledge, and understanding during and after some turbulent years. My husband Gary, Kristyn, and I had been experiencing anguish from past and present hurts. It's so sad but true—hurting people hurt others. External influences beyond our control had entered our lives, and none of us understood the impact those outside influences were having on the nucleus of our family until our lives had been turned inside out.

Anything that negatively affects one person can easily have a negative effect on another. Each decision we make is important, even if we believe our choices only apply to ourselves. Our choices will either affect or infect others, which can later come around to impact us as well. Without placing blame anywhere, kindness and thoughtfulness among members of our household would have gone a long way to support one another during our most troubled years. Kindness can help the thawing-out process in the hardest of hearts.

Letting God work in and through us will produce the best outcomes for any situation or circumstance. In giving every part of my life over to God (including my relationships), I found a peace that cannot be described in words.

This book began in June of 2008 with a simple yet loaded question that I felt driven to answer: "How did my garden grow?" After thousands of words had been poured onto paper, I realized the word *garden* needed to be plural. Life is filled with multiple garden plots as seeds are blown in and sown from various sources. I grew more than I've ever grown and learned more than I've ever learned as a result of following through with God's direct challenge to me.

I came to feel that direct challenge from God in two ways. First, while I was cleaning a dear friend's home, she asked a serious question that took me by surprise, "Do you have any faults?"

I didn't know how to respond; I just said, "Yes." The rest of the day, words to a poem started rising to the challenge. Words met me where I was at that day in time: "Mirror, mirror, tell me true. What do I see when I look at you?" The day was January 16, 2009. That's the day the poem "Reflections" was born. I began to look at myself through the eyes of a friend and realized she just saw the parts of me I allowed her to see.

The second challenge came from God while reading Psalm 26:2: "Put me on trial, LORD, and cross-examine me. Test my motives and my heart" (NLT). I prayed for God to open my eyes and heart to accept His will, in His way, in His time. You will find out after reading this book that He answered my sincere prayer.

When the gardens of the mind, heart, body, spirit, and soul are in alignment with the heartbeat of God, the harvest and fruits will be great. The gardens in life grow best when they are being tended by the Master of all gardeners, God Himself. I thank God that He set me free from all that held me in captivity and bondage for so many years.

"Astounding creativity kicks in when a great need develops."[1]
—Anthony H. Sinclair ("Tony")

Sore to Soar

’m not a journalist, yet I've grown to become a realist. We hurt ourselves more deeply when we choose to deny or devalue the existence of a person, place, or thing. There are times we may choose to deny something or somebody as a means of coping during a hurtful situation. When help is available and we choose to reject or push others away, we lose out on receiving blessings, help, and healing that our souls need. Indecisiveness blocks the flow of additional blessings and blocks our ability to live life more productively. Human pride, ignorance, self-preservation, and our need to control that which is out of our control become obstacles that can get in the way of personal success and daily fulfillment.

Keep It Shut: What to Say, How to Say It, and When to Say Nothing at All by Karen Ehman is what I call a keeper book, one I plan to reread on a regular basis. Truth, humor, and relatable stories keep my attention, and Ehman teaches valuable ways to interact with those who light the fire of offense, annoyance, and deep hurt within. Instilling James 1:19–20 into my heart and keeping it close in mind will help me be a better person as I let Jesus live through me in thought, word, and deed. It reads, "My dear brothers and sisters, take note of this: Everyone should be quick to listen, slow to speak and slow to become angry, because human anger does not produce the righteousness that God desires."

The following is an applicable passage from Ehman's book, *Keep It Shut:*

God intentionally orchestrated the relationships in our lives. He knew who would share your last name—or your four walls. Who would occupy a seat in your car pool or dwell in the house right next door. It didn't surprise him who would wind up as your in-law or be the one to teach your kids.

All the humans you encounter throughout the course of the day are "on purpose" people. God plopped them into your life for a reason.

These souls—whether they are of the easy-to-love variety or the scratchy sandpaper kind—can be used by God to mold, reshape, and sometimes stretch our souls as he perpetually crafts us into creations who are becoming more and more like his Son.[2]

Letting go of ourselves, taking courage, and allowing The Healer to touch the painful wounds of our past that interfere with good and healthy daily living is not only desirable, it's necessary. I came to the realization that I am incapable of abundant living without God's help, provision, loving-kindness, care, forgiveness, mercy, and grace. I do nothing to deserve the magnitude of love He gives, yet He sent His Son to die in my place so that I could enter into His presence and grow to love Him more. For that, I'm eternally grateful.

3/22/2020

The time came to go through the ten Bankers Box® storage boxes that held this books' contents. It could have been a grueling process, yet I was being very gentle with myself. Each box held painful parts of my life's journey. The second box I came to showed me how terrible my first writings were, but that was not the point. I was panning for gold—nuggets I needed to find in order to put perplexing parts of my life together for the better.

Wisdom is gained as we experience pain. We learn that if we keep moving forward, we can get through most anything life throws our way. Lessons are learned if we choose to become the student instead of trying to teach what we have not yet learned. Picking through tear-stained pages of the cathartic parts of this God-inspired mission was important to positively identify what had set up camp in the hearts of those I loved, and that included myself. I enjoy finding the silver lining and positive aspects in the stormy clouds of life. When life throws me lemons, I remember that it's best to use the bitter and sour in good ways, making the best of the situation. That helps make the hard things in life sweet!

A cabin entered my life in August of 2010 when it was a twinkle in my husband's eye. Breaking ground didn't happen until the following May. I watched the cabin's development from its beginning. The twinkle in Gary's eye grew into a big, needy baby, then it became a star teacher. We named it The Blest Nest Guest Haus. Tiny details are a huge part of the cabin, and it was a joy to share *our baby* with others.

Rebekah and Chris celebrated their first wedding anniversary (February 25, 2013) at The Blest Nest. During their stay, a glittery owl caught Rebekah's eye, and another owl made a deep impression in their hearts. The happy couple held both owls close in memory after their departure.

My dear friend Linda enjoyed the cabin eight months later with her sister. By then, the first two owls had multiplied into more owls! It was intriguing to Linda, and she wanted to know more about the owls. Linda learned that most everything at the cabin had a unique story.

It all began when we needed something to hang from the iron hook a blacksmithing friend made as a gift to bless the cabin. The perfect place for the hook was in a prominent location in the upstairs bathroom. One night, Gary and I were helping dear friends serve refreshments in their local store. As a thank-you gift, they let us pick out something from their store to put in the cabin. I let Gary choose. Out of all the choices he could have made, Gary came back with a small glittery owl because it captured his attention and could hang on the iron hook in the bathroom. His choice still makes my heart smile. The owners wanted to give us more, so they surprised Gary and me with another gift before we left—a large owl with feathers. It happily perched on top of a rustic cedar hall tree in the cabin's master suite.

Shortly after their stay at the cabin, Rebekah and Chris were browsing in a gift shop near their home. A green ceramic owl caught Rebekah's eye, and she felt compelled to buy it for the cabin as a thank-you gift. She imagined the owl sitting on the emerald-green granite countertops in the kitchen. My mind went into high gear as to where the owl could be placed, because there was no room for it on the countertop. The only possible place was behind the stovetop, but the base of the owl was too large for it to sit flush. After intently studying the owl and considering how I could find a suitable resting place for it, the owl's eyes seemed to have something to say to the cook or whoever happened to notice its presence.

In my search for something to hold the owl steady and secure, I found a scrap piece of oak handrail in the basement. It fit the space perfectly. After I carved the top of the handrail for the owl to rest upon, the green bird seemed content in its new home. While I was cooking, the owl was watching me. As I passed by the stove, the owl drew me in for a closer look. For three days, words to a poem percolated within my soul. I wondered what words the wise owl had to say! The beautiful ceramic owl inspired words to flow from my heart. This is what the Down-to-Earth Wise Owl said from its perfectly positioned perch:

Sittin' on a handrail made from oak, I'm quiet. Listen. I just spoke.
Whoooever takes the higher road brings to the table lighter loads.

Nature, children, and a host of art forms are star teachers if we stop our busyness long enough to be still, look around, and listen. The small voice of reason longs to teach us a lesson or two or more. God speaks to us in the most creative ways. Reach out and welcome God's loving embrace and rely on His perfect wisdom. It is there we will find peace only God can give, bringing rest to our tired and weary souls.

No matter what life brings, whether it be good or bad, I choose to be content. In the past, giving in to fear and doubt made situations worse instead of better. As I trust God 100 percent with any problem, issue, or concern, there is no room left for worrying. Doing things God's way works. When I pursued peace with a passion, God reached out and saved me from the helpless state of confusion and chaos that had hijacked my mind and infected my heart.

Unless an individual has personally experienced God's amazing love, grace, mercy, and forgiveness, there is no way for them to be understood or easily explained. While I was growing up, I practiced religion. Pursuing a real relationship with Jesus should not have been foreign to me, yet it was. I dressed up, sang hymns, heard sermons, prayed prayers, and attended church most Sundays and countless Wednesdays. It wasn't until many years had passed that Jesus became real to me; it was the time when I finally decided to be true to myself. Writing this book helped me discover and love the real Brenda, quirks and all.

The habits of love, kindness, encouragement, support, hope, peace, joy, patience, endurance, perseverance, determination, and a will never to give up, no matter what, can be caught by others as we live our daily lives. Helping others makes me smile. The assignment of writing a book in my fifties and sixties about my life and how my gardens grew has proven to be fulfilling and rewarding. It blesses my soul when people share stories of how my openness, honesty, and willingness to serve others helped them deal with their personal struggles.

Every person has their own opinions about subjects that may or may not matter to them. These opinions are based on personal beliefs, ideas, values, and life experiences. Freedom of speech and expression is a gift to be appreciated. Even though we may have differences of belief, opposing opinions, and various ways of doing things to obtain results that please us, there are two things every person has in common: each of us is human, and each of us has made—and will make—mistakes.

In giving one another room to breathe by choosing to treat one another fairly, respectfully, nonjudgmentally, and lovingly, we will grow wiser and stronger as we choose to give others the kind of treatment we long to receive ourselves. The scars we wear inwardly and outwardly reveal hurts that have become important parts of our beings. Memories tucked inside the scars are either unhealed or healed. In viewing each of my wounds one at a time, I became able to see them in a different light based on information I had since received as a student in the School of Hard Knocks.

When we allow another person's timetable for healing and wellness to dictate and control when we will get better, be better, or do better ourselves, we remain under the control and influence of another. To break free of those limits, we must be proactive and cease calling ourselves victims. Rising above the victim's stance to become victorious over something that is life draining takes the will of a humble heart and a mindset fixed on good things, determination, and fortitude.

God is using all the events, situations, circumstances, and people in my life to produce the person He meant for me to be—for His glory, not mine. Boasting about God's greatness affords me the freedom to expose my weaknesses and express myself without fearing attacks or condemnation. Knowing He has prepared the way for this book's birth gives me courage to share my heart openly and freely.

The sky's the limit for our imaginations, aspirations, and ideas. When we choose to point fingers, blame others, and give excuses for why we can't do something or have something, the fault is ours for saying, "I can't." Limiting ourselves to low standards cannot produce good results. We can't do anything worthwhile or of lasting value with that attitude. When we say, "I can," and still have doubts, we set ourselves up for potential failure. With that uncertain mindset and attitude of the heart, it becomes too easy to give up, give in, and settle for less than the ideal. However, when we say, "I can," with passion, purpose, belief, and persistence while holding on to a strong vision, we are encouraged to keep pressing on.

Appreciating every part of the journey toward a successful outcome can help us endure the hardships along the way and learn how to overcome difficulties that may arise. Blessings abound in ways that money cannot buy when we soar with wings of obedience to God, letting the Holy Spirit be our Guide, Pilot, Protector, Provider, Rescuer, Teacher, Healer, and Deliverer. The prophet Isaiah tells us that "those who hope in the LORD will renew their strength. They will soar on wings like eagles; they will run and not grow weary, they will walk and not faint" (40:31).

The most wonderful feeling of success comes after the most grueling of workouts. Working hard to rid ourselves of that which we unknowingly allow to control our minds and hearts is freeing, especially when a higher level of understanding is realized. With a deep sense of gratitude, we are then able to see how far we've come in our healing process. Gliding through life is much easier when we learn how to stay in our personal business and let others take responsibility for their actions or lack thereof.

Being a fixer and helper is not always well received. I'm still learning how to gracefully dance between responding to true needs, restraining myself so I won't enable, and backing off so I won't react inappropriately, which can create additional troubles. There are times when being a compassionate and attentive listener is all we need to do to send another person on their way intact. What we don't want to do is leave them feeling overwhelmed or attacked. Help others soar; it helps them purr, not roar! I love the way Karen Ehman sums it up in *Keep It Shut* (2015, 132): "We can't go wrong when we choose to obey Scripture."

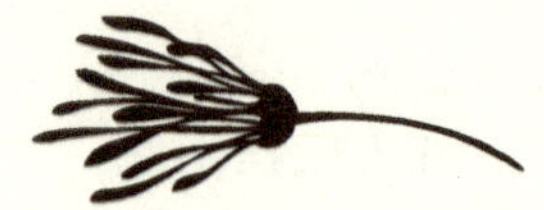

DEBASEMENT OR THE ROOFTOP?

The anchormen and -women on the earth report of news;
Some don't appear in media or get true funds for use.
To scatter and broadcast events from other people's lives
Is easy when those matters disclosed aren't about self's life.

We eat up what is juicy when news isn't about us;
That narrow beam of light requires a human to focus.
How would we feel if juicy news was tagged and bore self's name?
Would the spotlight highlight hurts we've had? Might news expose deep pain?

Would we participate and share so eagerly self's news?
Or would we wish that others had walked in our hard-soled shoes?
It's easy; folks will talk and share while chatting, oh, so free.
Since humans are so much alike, we share this tendency.

What could this wide world be like if *what's told is what is good?*
News flashes would be anchored by our love for brotherhood.
We humans have our weaknesses; let spotlights be on strengths.
What if our chatting sessions helped us think before we speak?

Each human heart controls each thought; be careful what mind plays.
What person's news will I report on this God-given day?
I'll choose to shine the spotlight on what others do that's right.
One can't go wrong when singing songs to help humans take flight.

Brenda Eller
3/7/2010

"Set a guard over my mouth, LORD; keep watch over the door
of my lips."

—Psalm 141:3

Little Things Matter

2013

During my dear friend's stay at The Blest Nest, Linda noticed something out of the ordinary. Later, curiosity emerged with these words: "Tell me about the rooster feather on the mirror in the downstairs bathroom. I want to hear its story."

To share the rooster feather's story, important background information must first be revealed.

Finding a bathroom light fixture to meet specific space requirements and please the designer/decorator proved to be a difficult pursuit—until the rooster light found me at the lighting store near our home. I wasn't looking for roosters to be a part of the cabin's decor. In the beginning, the rooster had no significant meaning to me. The first rooster came as a simple way to fulfill one of our lighting needs. After that initial investment, rooster decor seemed to call to me. My eyes were drawn to a rooster night light, rooster vinyl tablecloths, rooster kitchen towels, and rooster kitchen and breakfast-room curtains. I thought the rooster theme had been carried far enough. However, there would be more to come.

In the summer before I entered tenth grade, I met a young man named Phil. He was my first love, but a long-term relationship wasn't to be for him and me. We ended up going our separate ways before my senior year of high school. Shortly after the cabin was constructed, I was introduced to Rebekah and Chris at church. I didn't find out that Chris was Phil's son until later. This wide world continues to get smaller and smaller!

Before their anniversary stay at the cabin, Rebekah and Chris helped give a couples' baby shower for longtime friends. (Their friends were also members of our church, and they are the young couple who introduced me to Rebekah and Chris.) The shower was held at a nearby home, and I was invited. I knew the road well from my high school days yet wasn't familiar with the street address. After driving down the dirt driveway, I walked in through the home's open door. Rebekah greeted me in the breakfast room. Little by little, facts began to unfold like a flower blooming in due time. The reality was that Phil's two sons and their wives were in that home at the same time as me. Then Phil walked into the kitchen. At that moment, I realized it was Phil's home! Both of us were, without a doubt, surprised. After the baby shower, I learned about roosters, hens, and other feathery friends. Phil's backyard was an active feather haven. Standing outside the pen, I requested a rooster feather for the cabin.

Chris and Rebekah held my request in their hearts and kept in mind that little things do matter. I know that because before heading back to their home after celebrating their anniversary at The Blest Nest, they placed one rooster feather and three brown-and-white feathers on the kitchen's island for me to enjoy. It seriously blessed my soul. To me, the special brown-and-white feathers represented Chris and his two siblings. I chose to tuck them in above the "Angels Gather Here" plaque, where the three feathers could nest and rest together.

The rooster feather was placed in the bathroom to serve as a reminder that some experiences and outcomes are placed out of our reach because there's a better plan waiting to unfold. Being patient and not rushing into matters before their time can help us make wiser decisions. When life doesn't turn out the way we may have hoped, it's going to be okay because there are important lessons we must learn during that training/stretching/testing season. In order to grow into stronger, wiser, more conscious, vigilant, and courageous people, it's good to remember that pleasant memories can help us move on and let some things just be. Walking away in peace is not called "giving up." It's called "letting go for a good cause." And it's freeing. Being thankful for both the good and bad is soothing and calming and helps bring inner peace.

Divine foresight and intervention are seen in the tale and sheen of a rooster's tail feather. If Phil and I had married, his three children and my three children would not exist. Profound meaning was uncovered through one rooster's feather after it was shed. The feather wasn't plucked. Chris waited for one to fall to the ground after it was no longer needed by the rooster. It is inspiring when seemingly insignificant things turn into something significant and meaningful. Good memories cannot be bought, yet they can be experienced and shared. By illuminating the good surrounding us, we can observe beauty, charm, and love in the tiniest of details.

Reflecting on the rooster's tail feather inspired our Blest Nest guest Linda to inquire about how it had made its way to the cabin. The inquiry required me to do serious digging within. I didn't have to dig far to find out what the feather was really about. Enlightenment came as the pieces fell into place in the way, place, and timing God willed.

Reflections

"Mirror, mirror, tell me true.
What do I see when I look at you?"
Shy little girl, head tilted down,
Eyes looking forward to peer around.
Now in grade school, I still played with toys.
Liked the girl ones but became a tomboy.

Nailing steps on a tree to climb up so I could think.
Sat down on a branch with my apple juice to drink.
Making pies filled with mud, and breaking up small sticks;
The sticks became the candles for the pies so thick.

Playing in the woods on the tree swing-a-long,
I held on very tight and didn't even fall.
The Jack Rabbit Club then became the highlight.
My sisters, friends, and I made the rules so tight.

Making our own huts with the twisted vines so dense.
Spreading fresh pine straw made it comfortable to sit.
Ice cubes made from juice with napkins wrapped around.
We ate the "snacks" in our huts and didn't hear a sound.

Cereal boxes cut just right were flappers for my trike.
Later I secured them on my bright blue big-girl bike.
Flappers on the spokes were loud as I pedaled down the street.
The "motor" made me smile inside because it sounded sweet!

The carport was a place to play; we skated all around.
To adjust the skates for proper fit the skate key must be found.
The skates became the "wheels" under a seat made out of wood.
I rode my "go-cart" down the hill; sometimes it worked out good.

One day I felt so lonely; I didn't think anybody cared.
Decided I would run away, then started feeling scared.
A blanket made of flannel belonged to my boy doll.
I filled it up with candy for a trip that wasn't long.

While slowly walking down the street, I thought nobody saw.
My sister ran behind me, and then I heard her call,
"The ribs are on the grill; they'll be ready very soon!"
That sounded very soothing on this lonesome afternoon.

My hunger won me over; the candy had to wait.
I guess I shouldn't run away since I was only eight.
I got home and my family had eight eyes fixed on me.
Instead of grilled-out spare ribs, we were having black-eyed peas!

Disappointment set in quickly; tears fell from up above.
My family said, "We're sorry," then they showed me lots of love.
After eating black-eyed peas and yummy moist cornbread,
I unpacked all my candy, then I slowly crawled in bed.

I rode the yellow bus to school on mornings that were cool.
Afternoons would be such fun when I could leave the school.
While walking home in the afternoons, I'd stop at Mr. Jim's.
His service station was supplied with good ole chocolate milk.

Longneck bottles were so cold; they contained small chips of ice.
I savored each delicious sip; those short breaks felt so nice.
I kicked small rocks and pinecones with high-top tennis shoes.
Trees and brush were blanketed. "What lurked in that kudzu?"

Rocks and pinecones had to wait; I quickly upped my pace.
Kudzu looked so haunting. My heart began to race.
The pleasant scent of muscadine as I went around the bend
Reminded me I was almost home, then homework would begin.

Softball and basketball were played; I played on both the teams.
The second one was okay but it didn't make me beam.
My favorite sport was softball; the leather glove smelled good!
Shortstop, second base, and left field were places I once stood.

A home that we moved into had a special place to play.
I'd hide behind a pile of dirt that was filled with bright red clay.
Spoon and jackknife were my tools, and I carved out many roads.
Tiny figures from the five and dime fell down as toy cars rolled.

Our parents brought home Roman; he was fun and gave us hugs.
That doggie was my bestest friend—part boxer and part pug.
Roman's collar had a place that could hold a rolled-up note.
When needed, he would find us. The time was pre-cellphone.

Swimming in the pool was cool when the day turned into night.
Playing catch with Dad was fun, and I learned to fly a kite.
Another home, when I was twelve, intrigued with a trapdoor.
It led us to a cellar with an ice-cold cement floor.

First day of high school wasn't fun; it was all so new to me.
I couldn't find my first class, and the bell began to ring.
The hall soon cleared and was very long; I started walking fast.
The girls that year could not wear pants. I had to wear a dress.

My pace increased to running, and I hoped no one would see.
I rounded the corner. There it was. I almost skinned my knee.
An apple waited for me—shiny, big, and red.
With a pencil stuck right through it, I tripped and hit my head.

"Great way to start this day in a strange and brand-new place."
Head was fine but my feelings hurt; I then slowed down my pace.
It was hard to start all over then begin to make new friends.
I had to find my way in life and to see where I fit in.

It took two years to branch out; I tried out something new.
Trying out for the drill team was my break, long overdue.
Making cuts boosted self-esteem for three years in a row.
Treasured memories were made with friends I'm blessed to know.

Bright lights lit up the stadium, helping make my Friday nights.
Thirty shivering girls split up, stood still at goalpost lines.
We stood in short wool uniforms, awaiting "tweets" to sound.
They came in loud and clear; thirty boots then hit the ground.

Music from the marching band was heard well from behind.
Routines we practiced all week long were performed on day five.
Rewards were earned in three years; they made me long for more.
Great memories made years ago are permanently stored.

Engaged at eighteen, in love with love. Not much that I can say.
I'm sure if we had tied the knot, we'd be divorced today.
Went to college for one year then worked and lived with friends.
Those friendships I still cherish. They are true and will not end.

Reflecting on my early growth has set alight my mind.
I gained great insight tracking steps. They led me back in time.
Standing at the mirror waiting, my footprints come back to me.
Now we can walk together to be all we were meant to be.

Brenda Eller
1/16/2009

Early Sweet Seasons

We don't yet see things clearly. We're squinting in a fog, peering through a mist. But it won't be long before the weather clears and the sun shines bright! We'll see it all then, see it all as clearly as God sees us, knowing him directly just as he knows us! But for right now, until that completeness, we have three things to do to lead us toward that consummation: Trust steadily in God, hope unswervingly, love extravagantly. And the best of the three is love.

—1 Corinthians 13:12–13 MSG

Going to college full-time, while working part-time at a department store to cover expenses, wasn't for me. I managed to suffer through three quarters of taking classes such as literature, biology, accounting, and secretarial studies. I ended up dropping the biology and accounting classes. However, it was fun learning shorthand because I could write things that most people couldn't decipher. Then I spoke with my teacher about a desire to find a full-time job, and it was well received. Soon after our discussion, she informed me about a job opening near the college. Jumping on the chance to chart a new path created wonderful opportunities for personal growth.

Working full-time as a secretary at Sunkist Growers and going to school part-time made sense at first. However, that combination helped me realize I did not like school. Working long hours, driving for long distances, attending classes I didn't want to take, and doing homework I didn't enjoy made a hard decision easier. The reality was this: I was only going to college because it was what I believed other people expected of me. I was on my own to cover all of my college expenses. Paying for school a quarter at a time was keeping me out of debt. But I didn't like feeling forced to pay for something I didn't want to do. For twelve years of my life, I'd attended school because I had to. This time, I exercised my right to choose.

After completing the summer-quarter classes, I drove away and never looked back. No regrets. I'm not a quitter when it comes to most things, but the choice to cease doing activities that sapped joy and energy from everyday life was freeing and created a healthy new start to a new life.

Turning nineteen was welcomed, and my last year of being a teenager brought refreshing changes. My dear friend Carolyn was in need of a roommate. I was ready to get out on my own and was grateful for a job that paid enough to keep me afloat. Taking care of my 1971 red Capri coupe with a manual transmission—and a manual sunroof—made life pleasurable, as did listening to Carole King, the Carpenters, Bread, James Taylor, and Helen Reddy on the newly installed eight-track tape player. The cherry on the top was when our dear friend Sheri chose to move in with Carolyn and me, making our new family complete. Being a newly created family of three was a joy and a blessing. We worked well together and considered one another's interests above our own regarding who would take out the trash, who would use the washer and dryer, who needed the apartment for a date, and so on. We've remained treasured friends ever since.

During that summer, Gary was sharing his first apartment experience with my youth pastor. At twenty-three, Gary was ripe and ready for life now that he was out from under his parents' roof. With both of us working full-time, we found ourselves enjoying free time together with mutual friends. The person I was dating lived in the same apartment complex as Gary, and he was part of our friend group. Then the year wore on, and 1976 arrived. I was no longer dating anyone, and the twinkle in Gary's eye landed on me.

Our first date was January 31, and Gary behaved like a gentleman. On the drive to and from Crossroads Seafood restaurant on Peachtree Street in Atlanta (now closed), we shared likes and dislikes, hopes, visions, and dreams. Since I had a bad cough, Gary chose to cut our date short in his best effort to think of me instead of himself. He got an A+ by taking care of me in memorable and special ways. My well-being and health were important to him. I was shown that truth in actions when he stopped at a convenience store, bought cough syrup, and poured the cherry-flavored remedy into a spoon. It was so sweet, and I'm not referring to the cough syrup.

After he opened the car door for me at the restaurant, and when we arrived back at my apartment, I was already thinking I really liked this guy! He gave me a quick kiss at the door, and our first date was over. However, what he didn't know was that I closed the apartment door and leaned against it, deep in thought. Remembering the paper I had recently written, titled "My Man," I ran up the stairs to reread the qualities I had listed for the man worthy of being my husband and the father of my children. As I wrote the list, I had asked God to be in control of my dating relationships because I had not done a good job with discernment in the past. My desire to find a real-life version of "My Man" was pointing me in Gary's direction.

I wasn't ready to hear "I love you" as quickly as it came after our first date. I had drawn some boundary lines, needing to get to know Gary as a friend before we became serious as dating partners. The breathing space he gave me was welcomed. We enjoyed spending time together playing tennis, hiking, and looking at photos of our growing-up years. By the end of July, I was ready to start dating Gary seriously again. He gladly agreed, and our times together were enjoyed on a deeper level. I prayed a lot about our relationship and asked God to show me if the love we shared was the kind of love that lasts. I had never felt before the way I felt about Gary, and I wanted to be sure our love was real.

On November 28, I enjoyed a home-cooked meal in my apartment with Gary, Carolyn, and our new roommate, Triffy. Then something surprising took place after Gary and I sat on the couch. Without saying a word, Carolyn and Triffy swooped into the den, lit candles around us, selected "Nadia's Theme"[3] to play on the stereo, then quickly went upstairs. The mood had been set, but neither Gary nor I knew what was about to take place. Neither did they!

After we talked for a while, Gary began to restlessly swing his crossed leg up and down. His facial expression said, "I want to say something but don't know how to say it."

I cupped my hand under his chin and said, "Just spit it out."

He gave me a sheepish grin, and out popped these words: "I wouldn't mind if you were my wife."

I replied, "I wouldn't mind if you were my husband."

That was it! We were engaged. Gary wanted to let his friend the jeweler find me a special diamond. I received the engagement ring three months later.

Our engagement was a very serious promise we made to one another. Gary and I were once engaged to individuals who were not meant to be our spouses. Even though Gary didn't *ask* me to marry him, the question had been implied. That marked the beginning stages of our, oftentimes, awkward communication skills. We married on May 14, 1977. After we had celebrated "making it through many years of marriage," I popped a serious question to Gary. "Did you really ask me to marry you that night, or was it just a passing thought?" He confirmed with "Yes." He had seriously wanted to marry me. I needed to believe him, so I did.

Even though we thought we knew one another well before marriage, neither of us understood the magnitude of the marital decision. Our first surprise came when it was time to get a marriage license. Gary was astonished to learn I was only twenty years old. He thought I was older. I don't know how that important piece of information had been missed.

In the early seasons of marriage, the coffee pot was a fun place to connect via notes left for the other to find. Gary's job as a UPS tractor-trailer driver required him to work through the night, and I was getting home from work when he was leaving. Before coming home after work, Gary took naps in his 1977 blue Chevy pickup truck while tucked inside his sleeping bag. Then he would attend morning classes at college. Obviously, we didn't see each other much. Staying in contact during the days and nights required creativity. The first years of our marriage were positive, pleasant, and peaceful.

I have discovered that being sensitive to the emotions and needs of our loved ones will teach us how to care for them in meaningful and innovative ways. Appreciation, thoughtful acts of kindness, and sincere love can be freely given to our mates without us ever expecting anything in return. To me, that is the essence of romance. Little things are not little to the recipient of unconditional and genuine love. All the little things add up, and the additions are well worth the investment of time, energy, and creativity to make life better for those involved.

From 1980 to 1987, our family of two blossomed into a beautiful family of five. The local elementary school was closing, and there was not a public school option for our address at that time. We needed to either physically move or send the children to a private school. The one we could afford was in another county. When I found out I would have to wear a dress anytime I was on the Christian school's property, it became an easy decision; we chose to move.

The rental home we found was in a recreational location where bike paths were in abundance. We thought that would allow us to have plenty of fun while our new home was being built, and we did! Building a home was a huge undertaking, and we allowed each other to have input on the day-to-day decisions. However, our new home's blueprint didn't include a blueprint for what marriage was really about. In the fourteen months it took to build our new nest, it would have served us well to do individual and marital preparatory work to help us weather upcoming storms with grace. But we didn't know what we didn't know.

The decision to build a home arose from a need rather than desire. The targeted county was chosen because the school system was top-notch. When we couldn't find a home already built that would serve the needs of our family long term, a suitable lot was purchased and house plans were contemplated. With a builder in place and house plans chosen, we were set to go.

Well, not exactly.

To stop life in its tracks and call for a time-out is not realistic. Life doesn't work that way. What would we say in the huddle if we had the opportunity to put life on hold and regroup? Bucket lists can help individuals prioritize what is important to them so they can work toward fulfilling their goals and dreams. When Gary and I moved out of our comfortable singlehood lives into sharing life together as husband and wife, we honestly didn't know what we were doing. We just did what came naturally. That was mistake number one.

Successful marriages function best with a well-designed plan. When both partners know what that plan is and understand their individual roles, they are better equipped to willingly and sacrificially love and serve the other no matter what life throws their way. Building a strong and secure marriage requires more than saying vows and hoping for the best. Gary and I did quite well in our beginning stages of marriage. We were a cutesy young, carefree couple. Yet as time marched on, life became more and more complicated and challenging.

Timothy Keller wrote an amazing and heart-opening book titled *The Meaning of Marriage: Facing the Complexities of Commitment with the Wisdom of God*.[4] The gift of hindsight is a blessing. To become aware of and utilize the tools we have readily available is a great place to start, no matter where we are in life. Thankfully, the puzzling pieces of marriage have been put together in a relatable way by Keller, backed up by the wisdom and Word of God.

Keller's book was originally published on November 1, 2011, but I didn't know the book existed until October of 2020. That's when Alan Lewis, our caring, concerned, and prayerful friend, made me commit to reading a special book before he shared the book's title and author. I ordered the book, and Gary read it first. He summed up the book with these words: "It's like reading the owner's manual to your car." That was a huge compliment to the author. Keller's book contains life-changing wisdom that opened the floodgate of understanding for us. Thank you, Alan, for caring and sharing.

One of my close and dear sounding boards, Beverly, shared this pointed message regarding how to get along with others and maintain healthy relationships: "It all boils down to this: When we are daily walking in the Spirit, we are living out the fruits of the Spirit: love, joy, peace, patience, kindness, goodness, faithfulness, gentleness, self-control (Galatians 5:22–23 ESV). When each mate is doing their part, God is able to work in and through us. Otherwise, the wall of separation distances us from the power of God living and breathing through us. It's just that simple."

A marriage is not drought tolerant. When I water my husband, I am watering myself. And when my husband waters me, he is watering himself. I look forward to digging into this elective course I refer to as Marriage 101. Thank you, Dr. Keller, for helping us learn how to be patient with each other and help ourselves.

"The couples that are 'meant to be' are the ones who go through everything that is meant to tear them apart and come out even stronger than they were before."

—Anonymous

SOUL MATES ARE MADE

To have a soul mate, one must be a soul mate in return.
Two temperaments will aim to please; souls dance instead of churn.
Accommodate. Adapt to fit. Agree to disagree.
Appropriate responses help to meet each other's needs.

A give + give mentality, summed up, will bless, not test.
A give + take does not add up—steals love, joy, peace, and rest.
True kids can have fun all day long in a playground called the mind.
Adults can have that same playground and imagination find!

It's in there waiting to be found; each self must find its own.
The simple life and simple joys build happy nests in souls.
To give away, we must first have an accepting love of self.
Be a best friend to the entire self, then your soul mate you can help.

Give smiles away; they travel miles. Frowns dig in on both sides.
See comedy, not malady; humor smooths bumpy rides.
Be sure to tell and show soul mate love freely through the days.
Short lives and days are numbered; make acts count in real-life plays.

Positives are great to leak; let soul mates hear good thoughts.
Appreciate through gratitude. Affirm; it bears no cost.
Approve with honesty. Respect. Be true and never fake.
Allow God's love to permeate. It's sure to bless soul mates.

Soul mates can come in different ways,
Through marriage and best friends.
Keep polished heavens' friendships.
Gratitude should never end.

Brenda Eller
1/13/2010

Infestations of Home and Heart

Having been a homeowner for most of my married life, I've been forced to learn about various bugs and pests as well as the numerous ways they can interrupt and interfere with normal living. The houses my family and I have lived in proved to be valuable teaching tools for me as I endured lessons and assignments that tested and stretched me in unimaginable ways. Experiential learning is the method that captures my attention and teaches me best. A painful yet important class I attended at the School of Hard Knocks required me to learn more than I ever cared to know about bugs and pests.

Most every home we have owned had a unique set of problems that needed to be addressed. Thanks to my hardworking and dutiful husband, I was given the highest honor and privilege of being a stay-at-home mom. Since he was the one working hard to take care of us financially, I was the one to tackle the many unpleasant happenings that have crept into our lives in the craziest of ways.

Several local exterminators nicknamed me "the Bug Lady" as a result of the following nightmarish occurrence that interrupted the peace in my household, heart, and mind. On August 28, 1992, I learned that enemies had been residing in our dream home, which had been completed in 1990. In the quietness of that day, I heard a ticking sound, which made me suddenly stop and remain still for a moment. As I listened more intently, I heard the same sound coming from a different place. Concern began to creep in, and I asked myself, "What is that noise?" The ticking of the kitchen clock was also heard, but the sound wasn't coming from the clock. My inner alarm sounded, and I sensed a problem that needed immediate attention.

My investigative nature set me on a mission to discover the source of the ticking sounds. Since the sounds were faint and I wanted to listen carefully, I searched Kristyn's bedroom for the toy doctor's kit, which contained a stethoscope that really worked. After a six-foot ladder was brought into the dining room, I was ready to proceed with the investigation. If a casual observer could have seen me at that moment, it would have been quite comical to see an adult standing on a ladder listening to a dining room ceiling with a child's stethoscope!

But all joking aside, our family was facing the most difficult year we had encountered until that point. The stethoscope allowed me to hear the ticking sounds in addition to a new type of sound similar to that of mice gnawing on wood. Since the sounds were coming from the area between the first and second floors, the only thing these pests could possibly be chewing on was our home! My innermost being became seized with fear of the unknown.

Numerous exterminating companies were called upon to assess the situation the following week. My concerns grew stronger when several of the professionals believed it could be the old house borer (OHB), which is the only beetle in the Cerambycidae family of 1,800 that would reinfest if all stages of the beetle's life cycle were not fumigated and destroyed. I was warned of the hardship our family would be facing if this was in fact the OHB.

With renewed determination and intensity, the investigation continued as I called upon my dad to help. The goal of this mission was to find the enemy so that I could determine what course of action to take next, if any. My never-give-up mindset drove me to track down one of the enemies that had invaded our home. Disassembling Kristyn's bedroom was necessary since it was directly above the dining room, where the sounds were coming from. My dad helped me by removing a large portion of her carpet and flooring, revealing several piles of a fine yellowish powder (which we later learned was called *frass*). Also found were several one-fourth-inch oval exit holes in some of the eight-by-ten floor joists. This was a vital finding because the life cycle of the OHB is two to six years from the time eggs are laid until the adult beetles emerge.

Our search proved to be successful. The tunnel of one of the enemies suddenly became visible when a portion of the subfloor was pulled away from a joist. Fully exposed in all of its glory was a living inch-long larva! My excitement continued as I preserved the little guy or gal in a glass jar containing 70 percent isopropyl alcohol.

The next step was to get the specimen examined. Since our children and I enjoyed going on field trips of our own choosing from time to time, I decided to create a memorable trip for us by hand-delivering the larva for examination instead of mailing it. This particular field trip consisted of our three children, the unidentified larva, and me traveling to a well-known state university to meet with the head entomologist. Several exterminators had been correct from the onset. After examining the larva under the microscope, the entomologist confirmed that "it was indeed the larva of an Old House Borer." He volunteered to be my expert witness in court if needed. With the validation and support of an expert in the field of entomology, I didn't feel alone in this fight for what was right.

The reality of this newfound knowledge began to invade my thoughts in an attempt to overshadow and steal this special time I got to spend with our children. Thankfully, during those precious moments, I was unaware of the lengthy and distressing battle I would soon be forced to painstakingly fight. Better judgment directed my focus toward our children and the homecoming parade that had just begun on campus. After watching the parade, we enjoyed a picnic and headed back to Bugsville with the OHB preserved in a tiny professional specimen jar.

***

The fumigation process was an experience I would love to erase from my memory, yet that is impossible. We had no other choice than to fumigate. Preparing our home for the fumigation required its contents to be evaluated as to whether they could remain in the house during the gassing process. Furniture and furnishings could stay. Going through drawers, closets, storage spaces, toy boxes, basement, and attic meant that anything that could trap gas inside had to be opened to allow it to escape. Preparing the kitchen area was like we were moving.

In addition to preparing our home indoors, we needed to temporarily relocate some plants that were near our home's foundation so the entire exterior could be wrapped, tented, and sealed with plastic. A cherry picker/bucket truck was used for the workers to wrap the highest parts of the house. The goal was to have an airtight seal so the poisonous gas could permeate every part of our home. Sand was distributed on the plastic around the perimeter of the house to ensure gas could not escape.

For obvious reasons, it was necessary to seek temporary lodging elsewhere. We deeply appreciate Gary's parents allowing our family to stay in their home until it was safe to reenter and reoccupy ours. Like a ghost, poisonous gas went through walls, studs, joists, flooring, and everything under the sealed plastic tent. After the gas dissipated, when the airtight seal was cut and the gas was at zero parts per million, we could safely reenter. No living creature could have survived being exposed to eighteen hours of the gas fumigant. After the gassing, the airtight seal was left undisturbed for an additional eighteen hours. Those bugs were history!

Even though the fumigation company had given us permission to enter, my heart began to race as I stood at the front door knowing what had recently taken place. All of the exterior doors were locked and still had the "Danger/ Poison Gas" signs displayed with their skull-and-crossbones pictures. It was disconcerting not to feel safe entering our home even though we had been told it was safe to enter. I had to trust and believe the professionals. While holding my breath, I went in and opened the nearest window. Breathing fresh air was a relief. Holding my breath had been the only way I could cope with that fear of the unknown. I began to relax and realized I hadn't died. Trusting the words of those professionals turned out well.

We moved back in, yet the hardest fight of my life was still before me and would require everything I had to give and more. There was no time to put off the battle for financial restoration. The fumigation had been costly, and we later discovered more costs would be incurred.

This fight for justice led me to a wonderful story line for this book! The life cycle of bugs, pests, and intruders parallel in amazing ways the issues that can wreak havoc in human hearts and lives and tear relationships apart. Our homes are part of our life gardens that can be damaged, disrupted, or destroyed when the enemy enters and works silently until signs of its presence are felt, heard, and seen.

If the larva I found had been one of the other 1,799 types of beetles in the Cerambycidae family that do not reinfest after emerging, this chapter of my life would not have been important. All it took was one documented OHB larva that changed the real-life game for me. One male or female OHB larva was one too many, yet I had proof that there were more. None of them were welcomed in our home. They all had to go!

As I put on the hat of an investigative reporter and learned about particular legal matters, the tasks ahead demanded I be knowledgeable about when the infested wood was delivered to our property and to know more about the OHB than some exterminators. Thankfully, I had taken photos of the different stages of our home's development from its beginning until completion. On the back of photos, I had written the dates when major milestones were achieved. The flight season of the OHB is in June and July. The delivery date for the lumber was in August, which proved that the microscopic OHB larvae (plural) were already in the wood before being delivered to our property. Being able to prove something beyond a shadow of a doubt is crucial in order for the evidence to stand up in a courtroom. I sensed that was where this case was headed, and I made certain to cross my t's, dot my i's, stick to the facts, and stay a step ahead of everyone else involved.

After my attorney sent a demand letter to the president of the mill where the infested lumber was purchased, the mill's president seemed to know it was best to settle out of court to make me go away. I was a nice gnat, yet I was firm and clear in stating facts and making requests. Prayers, perseverance, determination, and tenacity were utilized. However, it is God who will always get the glory for this victory. He already had the tiniest of details covered!

Here is a great example. Our builder graded the lot in May of 1989. Then he needed to put a hold on our build until he finished building his personal home. The OHB's flight season for emerging and laying eggs was during the time the construction of our future home was on hold. The lumber was delivered after the flight season, not during it. That delay protected us. It allowed the contents of the brown paper grocery bag filled with evidence to clearly speak and support my case. The president of the mill must have realized his odds of winning this battle in court were slim to none. Eleven long months later, he reimbursed us the total amount of all submitted receipts. He finally did the right thing and I will forever be grateful.

My first garden plot was a dream long before our dream home turned into Bugsville. Using a mattock and hoe to cultivate raw land was labor intensive and hard on my back. It didn't take me long to give up on that method of cultivating the garden plot. I began dreaming of owning a tiller. After the president of the mill sent me a check for everything related to the OHB case, we did some of the repairs ourselves. With the extra funds available, I bought a six-horsepower rear-tine tiller and several quality kitchen knives. I definitely deserved and earned those amazing gifts. My hard work had paid off. We put Kristyn's room back together and tried to get back to everyday normal living, whatever that looked like.

Through this first experience of having to fight hard for something that I couldn't allow to run us over, I learned I had the guts and fortitude to face giants with God's help. In looking back through my life, the years of 1992 and 1993 were monumental years for me. Those were the years that my *not-giving-up* and *not-giving-in* mindsets first emerged. I didn't realize that was in me, yet that attitude has helped me fight for what was right countless times. Rolling over and giving in is not a part of who I am. As trying and disturbing as the OHB battle was, God helped me see blessings He had kept hidden until I could fully acknowledge and appreciate those extra-special gifts.

Enhance to Dance

3/22/2020

At the time it was penned, I didn't understand how important the following letter from me would become in putting the pieces of our marriage together. The letter was written to my love, Gary, on May 22, 2009. Discovering this golden nugget was significant as Gary and I looked back over our married life.

After rereading the letter ten years and ten months later, Gary asked, "Do you know what happened in 1990?"

I replied, "Yes, that's when we moved into our newly built home."

He continued. "What else?"

"That's when you went into business development at work."

"Exactly. That's when the notes you referred to in the letter stopped."

Insight had arrived, and I said, "That's when core borer eggs in our relationship were laid."

(Note: The change in Gary's job involved a move from an operations management position to one in corporate business development. That change consumed his time and energy and coincided with eight years of completing his undergraduate and graduate degrees.)

We never know how drastically the decisions we make can alter lives until the roots of truth become unearthed and exposed. Letter writing is a creative way I found to express my thoughts and feelings. I hope that you will experience my heart and clearly see the impact of our decisions in the following letter, written to my husband at the beginning of our restoration.

5/22/2009

My Love,

The feelings that we have held at *bay leave* much work that needs to be done in our marriage. I am inviting pleasant thoughts of you to *cumin* to my mind so that I'll never be too busy, too mad, too tired, or too distracted to focus on the needs of my man, the one God created to be my partner for life.

Love is waiting to be awakened. I will leave nothing to chance. Negative and biting words came into our marriage and depleted love banks that were once filled with *allspice.* The tender, compassionate, thoughtful, validating, kind, and loving man that I married is back with me today. I am so grateful that we found each other again.

Forgiveness has been offered for the *rue* (regrets and sorrows) that has infiltrated our lives. It has been forgiven by God, by us as a team, and as individuals. All parts of the past happened; they are done. Today we are miraculously still together and are now beginning on the same page, from this day forward, with Jesus being at the center of our lives and our marriage.

Every day, I will be intentional in making each gifted day better than the day before. In addition to *sage* being a well-known and loved seasoning to enhance the flavor of food, "sage" also refers to someone who has attained wisdom. Sage ones have grown wiser and more prudent with each life experience, whether the experiences are positive or negative. Reflecting on certain events and mistakes enables the wise to learn and exercise good judgment in their behaviors, responses, and words. We are there now; our inner gardens have produced two sage people who have learned much from our pasts. Always learning and always growing, I will be loving you.

I remember the thirty-six-foot-by-fifty-six-foot vegetable garden at our other house in the 1990s. I'm sure you do! Thank you for supporting me as I enjoyed tilling my first garden plot, where I had to remove huge rocks that were in the way of progress. Using our hand truck and plywood to move each rock one by one was a feat in and of itself. Do you remember the time I drove our straight-shift blue pickup truck to a barn on a farm? I hand shoveled a truckload of composted horse manure and shavings, then tilled it into the freshly cultivated garden soil at home.

It is amazing how manure from certain animals can be so beneficial in producing a good harvest from which humans can obtain nourishment. The pole beans enjoyed hanging out on their bamboo teepees until they were picked. Bush beans, lettuce, okra, corn, squash (yellow and zucchini), tomatoes, cucumbers, and peppers flourished in the well-prepared soil. You were at work when our children, nephews (Travis and Jarrod), and I made chow chow pickled relish one hot summer day. Fond memories of that summer day are so sweet! Bucket after bucket of produce was harvested and brought into the kitchen. Each child helped me cut up the garden goodies. It was long, tiring work. However, it was rewarding when we got to enjoy the fruits of our labor.

I could bring that story of long ago back to us when our life together was as if "refuse from others" was being tilled into our hearts and home, one painful shovelful at a time. I'm sure you can remember the hurtful expressions, belittling words, and critical remarks that came from many directions and sources. You and I were deeply affected in negative ways and didn't know how to deal with it properly or in healthy ways. Each pile of hurts became larger and larger in our hearts. As the hurt, pain, and pressure in our lives built up and became mixed with other things of significance, it all began to heat up and over time broke us down.

With the 20/20 vision that humans have in hindsight, I am actually grateful for all that was thrown into the mix. It stunk then, but it has now reaped a bountiful harvest of joy in our hearts. We came through that and are still standing together! Leaving the manure behind and instead focusing on enhancing our marriage, I understand that **peppers** stimulate the senses. They can either be hot, mild, or sweet and come in different colors (red, green, yellow, and orange). As your mate and lover, I am making the conscious choice to sprinkle, season, and cover you with good and positive actions and words that are gentle, compassionate, and loving that will serve to benefit you and stimulate your senses. Since we discussed this at length after we realized we needed to make changes, I trust and believe that you will do the same for me.

You and I both know what can happen to a marriage when negative actions, behaviors, and words are directed toward a mate. The mate becomes unnerved and defensive. Instead of senses being stimulated, they become inflamed yet deadened. The weeds of bitterness and resentment take over to choke and entangle.

I am so thankful we are in the place we're in now and have both agreed to do what is essential to revive our marriage instead of continuing to let it move toward a slow and painful death. Taking our marriage from blah to hurrah is my goal and intent.

Do you remember the single rose I excitedly picked out for you as a surprise? And then, after its life was spent, how you came to me holding the flower, asking, "How can I preserve this?" It brings a smile to my heart remembering those special moments when I view the flower in our china cabinet today. Your rose is snuggled up in a vase next to a rose that you gave me! They are a good visual of us as one.

Like the pleasure that is derived from the gift of a single **rose, mary** me all over again, please? God created the institution of marriage to season our lives with blessings and nourishment that God has in store for us. I want, more than anything, for our marriage to follow God's design, which is our blueprint for victory straight from our Creator. We will need His help daily because we know it is impossible to be our best when we rely on our own selves. The recommitment of wedding vows can do wonders to jump-start our marriage, which has suffered long enough with a dead battery. Let's begin again and follow God's lead 100 percent from this day forward.

Salt and **pepper** complement each other and make a great pair. It is proper at a dining table that when one requests the salt, the pepper is passed too and vice versa. The pair are together even when they are apart. This is how I want us to be, a healthy and together pair. We have been in our own worlds for way too long, not giving proper consideration to the needs or interests of each other.

It is a blessing to get to read notes and cards we exchanged in the early sweet seasons of our marriage. Thankfully, I was able to locate them in the basement. The notes and letters you wrote to me became a key to jog your memory since you told me you couldn't remember the way we were when we began our marriage and started our family.

Dating again is fun and exciting! Reflecting on our roots and beginning helped us remember why we married in the first place. The habit of loving each other unconditionally got lost in the complexities of life. Just as a gardener must prune the dead and ineffective branches to stimulate new growth, our Master Gardener has been pruning you and me. It hurt badly for many years, but it was through the challenging and painful times that we've grown the most.

Since life is full of change, all days are not the same; they will differ greatly as we age. ***Summer savory***, and some are not! We will both have difficult, stressful, and low days. Going forward, I choose to be quick to forgive, do my best to ignore petty irritations, be patient when I feel wronged, and attentively listen as you share your heart with me. It is now our ***thyme*** to thrive, not just survive. I am excited to begin again with you as we dance through life together as one, allowing Christ to take the lead. My man, I love you!

Love, Wifee
P.S. It is wise for us to release all ***caraway*** into the hands of God.

KIND-LING TO KINDLING

Be a "KIND-ling" to your earthly mate.
Rewards build hearts that will not break.
When the focus is set on what is right
The ties that bind are good and tight.

When the heart is bent on what is wrong,
Coldness will win, and pride reigns strong.
With feet dug in to win the war
New enemies are now keeping score.

Lovers still, it takes two to fight.
God's design for marriage—this cannot be right.
Desiring and deciding to cease the war.
Crave peace and rest. There must be more.

When I searched to find God's perfect way,
He did not disappoint. These are all His new days.
Life's journey found us on dry, rocky roads;
The burdens were heavy as we carried our loads.

Defenses torn down, they're put out of our minds;
We opened heart doors and drew the straight line.
What's done has been done, never saying, "The End."
We chose to start dating all over again!

Many years had tugged, tried to pull us apart.
We're so thankful each day for a vibrant fresh start.
Glowing fragments left over from long-ago fires,
Enlivened by kindness, helped us both to leap higher.

Staying close together instead of smoldering away,
We'll fan our new flame as we dance, love, and play.
Being soul mates forever is the desire of our hearts.
Kindling now in its place, ardent love must not part.

Brenda Eller
4/20/2009

Good Workouts

In the season of raising, training, and disciplining our three children, situations would present themselves in which we needed to give hard but useful advice and sometimes tough love. One particular instance was when our son Jeff committed himself to a long-term task. Soon, he realized he wanted to bail from that trail and choose a different path.

Jeff called us in tears and wanted so badly to come home to remove himself from the painful situation. Gary encouraged him to complete the short-term portion first. Then he could come home and rethink his plan of action. The situation was hard for us as parents to witness, yet it was especially tough for our son. However, Jeff grew stronger and wiser as a result. He focused on the goal and successfully endured the heavy burden.

There have been many situations during which I needed to stay the course until a particular goal was accomplished. One of those times was when our septic drain field lines were purposely diverted to another location so a new lawn could be installed. A beautiful, enormous oak tree had to be unearthed. Gary found out about it when he came home from work to find the massive tree, stump and all, in a horizontal position across the front yard. The dumpster in the street let him know that I had hired helpers to push over the tree so it could be completely removed. All was well. It was an important part of the process called "progress."

Instead of focusing on that temporary eyesore, I directed my attention toward preparing for a beautiful sodded lawn. I had the physical capabilities, knowledge, desire, and tools, including my trusty helper—the six-horsepower rear-tine tiller. Erosion control was a vital need to be addressed, and that required me to study the stormwater's path during heavy rains. With the street being the highest point of reference, I would be correcting problem areas from the highest point and working my way down to the sidewalk. Knowing where to add dirt and where it needed to be removed was imperative for the project to be given a good grade. Before the landscaping could commence, however, the old sidewalk needed to be removed and a wider one poured in a different place. Sounds simple, right?

From past experiences, I knew, if I wanted something done the way I envisioned, I needed to do the work myself. Installing a sidewalk was not within my areas of expertise, and I had to trust that the sidewalk would be done correctly. Unfortunately, I was not prepared for what took place as it was being installed.

Based on the location of the sidewalk, the steep driveway, and the slope of the front yard, the cement truck had to park on the street. Back and forth, the earthmover carried cement in the front-end loader from the street to the sidewalk forms. I tried not to let my face reveal what I was really thinking as I watched. Cement blobs were being dribbled wherever the earthmover traveled. The blobs dried quickly and became mixed in with roots from the tree-extraction project. Ruts from the earthmover made the damp red clay look like a red ocean with frozen waves.

The newly installed sidewalk was aesthetically pleasing and looked exactly the way I had envisioned. I was grateful we had a new sidewalk but was disheartened with the extra work that particular professional dumped on me. I learned that picking up the pieces he left behind was a forced way to practice patience. After all, what did I expect would happen when wet cement was being carried in an open container over uneven ground? I won't forget that science lesson!

I was ready to tackle the project of creating art in the front yard. Gary was willing to pay professionals and get the work done in a timely manner, but I needed to complete this massive undertaking myself. The driving force behind my decision to do it myself was for personal sanity and also for the well-known therapeutic benefits of gardening. Gary eventually gave me his promise that he would allow me to do this hard work all by myself without interfering in any way. I greatly appreciated that freedom.

After the red ocean was skimmed and cleared by hand, I could move forward with the fun parts of the work. Playing in freshly delivered topsoil reminded me of being a kid. That smell was divine! My friend the tiller made the work enjoyable. Neighbors began to ride and walk by, giving me thumbs-up approvals, smiles, and words of encouragement. After seventy-plus tons of topsoil had been mixed with the subsoil, I was ready to fertilize the dark "lawn" and lay the lush green sod. The rewards and sense of pride after that hard year of work were indescribable.

As I went through fitness training and soul therapy in the front yard, God had been gently whispering words of hope into my unsettled heart. Jesus said, "Come to me, all who labor and are heavy laden, and I will give you rest. Take my yoke upon you, and learn from me, for I am gentle and lowly in heart, and you will find rest for your souls. For my yoke is easy, and my burden is light" (Matthew 11:28–30 ESV). I thank God for the delightful and refreshing workouts. He knew I needed them—just what the Master Trainer and Therapist ordered!

The Sweet-Rocks Garden

"Motivation is when your dreams put on work clothes."[5]

—Benjamin Franklin

Standing on our former driveway looking at unraked leaves in the backyard, I knew what was hidden underneath. The leaves made messiness look beautiful. Weather-beaten compacted soil, sprawling tree roots, moss, and weeds were things I could see even though they were blanketed by leaves and out of sight. The problematic backyard compelled me to look upward momentarily.

Dense and beautiful aged hardwoods were a sight to behold. As the designated landscape designer at our then-current home, I was energized by the thought of bringing life into the backyard. I longed for an oasis where one didn't exist. However, no matter how difficult it might be or how much it might cost, I was not deterred from dreaming.

The dream began in June of 2008. It became necessary to have some trees removed and others thinned out so grass could have a fighting chance at adequate sunlight. Previous homeowners had left behind an untidy heap of ancient-looking bricks around a sweet gum tree. The tree stood in the way of progress and needed to come down.

Repurposing the bricks became a creative way to get them off the property and into the loving hands and hearts of children. Messy Camp at church was quickly approaching, and I was in charge of crafts. The bricks would make perfect doorstops for the children to paint and decorate. Scrubbing each brick was necessary, and I enjoyed the process as I brainstormed ways I could "paint and decorate" the backyard.

Contemplating what to plant and what type of patio to choose, I pursued the project with deep thought and a passionate sense of purpose. Even though the "softscape" work in the front yard was completed without needing to ask for help, the hardscape in the backyard presented greater challenges than I could physically handle.

Then it came to me—I could plant rocks! A multilevel stone patio would be an effective way to deal with the sloping yard and provide a comfortable place to relax and enjoy the beautiful surroundings. As if I were being pulled by a magnet, I got out of the chair where I was sitting and cleaning bricks and walked toward the backyard. The bricks, bucket, water, soap, scrub brush, and hose would be there when I returned. While standing on the edge of the driveway, I prayed over the backyard and what the next steps should be.

In my gardening life, I try to choose plants that don't need me to keep them alive. Rocks are drought-proof, deer-proof, weed-proof, pest-proof, and Brenda-proof. Planting rocks became the perfect solution! The fallen leaves were a handy way to mark the future patio's outline without spending a penny. Since I enjoy the curves in free-flowing patios, I chose to create curves using a garden rake, leaves, and my imagination. I followed a wise piece of advice: plan for a larger patio than what I believed we needed. Spare water hoses took the place of leaves in marking the future patio's shape before the leaves could be displaced by the wind. Then I used a mattock to dig a boundary line around the lengthy hose.

During this outer growing season, something new was also growing within. Although I didn't know it then, a seed had been planted in my heart as I stood on the driveway dreaming about the future patio while planting rocks in my mind. As if it were an invisible neon sign, I saw the words *How Did My Garden Grow?* That's when this book was conceived. I didn't know what those five words meant, yet God knew. That night, pent-up words surprised me as they began to flow . . . and flow . . . and . . . flow.

A family friend got the patio started by grading the site, helping select and deliver the awesome flagstones and rubble stones, and positioning huge stone steps to nest and rest together. His hard work became a wonderful beginning for what was to be. Then it was my turn. I chiseled away until the shape and depth of the subsoil made me smile. After I laid down my tools and picked up the phone, stonemasons from J. L. Rios Masonry came to the rescue. Jorge and his craftsmen masterfully completed the gigantic 3-D flagstone puzzle, which is breathtaking.

Messy Camp was messy, and so was creating a private backyard retreat in a deeply neglected and needy yard. The project took a year from start to finish, but once it was completed, the work of art was ready to be enjoyed by many. Memories of the peaceful flowing stream at the rear of the property and the oasis God created in my soul continue to be held near and dear.

Chiseling Georgia red clay after gentle rains was like carving a huge plaque using outdoor tools. Peering through the windows at the unchiseled, unlaid stone waiting patiently on their pallets felt like looking into a mirror at the messiness, heaviness, and confusion in my soul. The patio was completed in November of 2009, nine months after my healing journey began. (You will read more about that journey soon.) I needed to be part of this inspiring and important creation called the Sweet-Rocks Garden. Being a small part of making a big dream come true required much, yet it continues to give back in abundance.

"A thing of beauty is a joy for ever."[6]

—John Keats

A STONEMASON'S HEART

Stonemason I'm not, but I will try
To build these patios before winter is nigh.
The rough-in is formed. It's now being leveled;
An amateur I am with my mattock and shovel.

Additional tools to help with this task
Were specifically purchased, but I had to ask.
The questions I had were patiently answered;
Approval was received for this project to be mastered.

Persistent I am, and lazy I'm not.
The weather is perfect; the temperature's not hot.
Days can be long with my back brace on.
The pleasing anticipation spurs me along.

The leaves are falling but do not affect me;
My Maker's handiwork is all I can see.
Rubble stones and flagstones are patiently waiting
To express the heart of the artist's painting.

The female artist is neither man nor machine;
God sent me a man who made his earthmover sing.
Tons of stone he moved like a feather,
Will be strong enough to hold up in all types of weather.

The importance of leveling the subsoil is key,
Preventing the stones from settling.
Slight pitch of the site before exposure to rain
Will allow the excess water to drain.

THE SWEET-ROCKS GARDEN

While the earth is still fresh and the rains pour down,
Plastic on the dirt kept my face from a frown.
The sun comes out; the dirt starts to dry.
I put on work clothes then tell my friends, "Hi!"

My friends are the stones stacked up in the yard;
While facing me, they ask if the work is too hard.
I tell them honestly, "I enjoy every part.
The learning of 'How To' was the best place to start."

Digging the trenches before building the walls
Needed to be right to prevent future falls.
Chipping some stones to help them all fit
Will create special places for people to sit.

The stones all look happy, I'm proud to say.
I overheard them whispering, "We're here to stay!"
My Maker, who masterfully inspired this art,
Has created in me a stonemason's heart.

Brenda Eller
11/5/2008

The Better Business Boundary

3/5/2009

When I was in the sixth grade, my two sisters and I shared a bedroom. I slept on a double bed with my older sister, Beverly. Most of the time it didn't bother us because we got along so well. However, there were times we each didn't want the other to cross the imaginary line in the center of the bed. Encroaching on one another's personal space interfered with our peaceful rest.

Beverly had a six-foot-long stuffed snake that was covered with colorful yarn. The snake had cute eyes and a red tongue made from felt. It was pleasant, not scary. It came in handy when we needed to accentuate the boundary line at bedtime. Each night we would place the snake between us on the bed to ensure that each of us could enjoy our protected space. In the mornings, the snake was placed with the other stuffed animals at the head of the bed.

"Boundary, what's that?" became the question I started asking myself at fifty-plus years of age. It was about time! I had lived over half a century, was married, had raised three children to adulthood, and suddenly realized the essential nature of setting and keeping personal boundaries. This is quite humbling to admit.

Another question I asked myself was "Whose territory am I in anyway?" Judging hearts and the motives of others is God's business. I decided I needed to leave God's business to Him. Then comes the business of others. When able-bodied people, who should be stepping up and taking responsibility for their own choices, continue on their cyclical paths, it can drive us into making unwise decisions concerning them that will ultimately affect us. (A person is on a cyclical path when they want things to change in their life, yet they continue to do the same things, which keeps them from moving forward.) However, when *we* come back to reality and stop traveling *our own* cyclical paths, we are able to step up and take responsibility for our choices, leading us to make better decisions. Behaving in this manner can stop us from moving ahead of God and prevent us from jumping into places we might not need to be—but feel pulled to anyway due to our natural tendencies to want to help.

I've been on cyclical paths before. I call them the merry-go-rounds of insanity, which are not very merry. Doing the same things over and over again, expecting different results, does not bring about change. The only change we can control is how we choose to think and what we believe. This controls the words we allow to roll off our tongues and the deeds that are born in our hearts and come out as actions. Trying to fix something to make life easier or better for another often has a boomerang effect. Sometimes, no matter how well intended our acts of generosity and kindness are, we end up taking the heat when we are just trying to help someone not hit a brick wall or drown in their ocean of troubles.

I sought professional help to learn how to give tough love to someone caught up in a cyclical path. The advice the therapist gave was specific to the situation presented. The therapist's suggestions worked out well and sparked changes in the other party that needed to be ignited. The tough part of love tore at my soul, yet it was necessary. If a person is struggling with how to give tough love in helpful ways, seeking professional help to learn how to navigate through unfamiliar territory is a wise decision indeed. That, in fact, is true regarding anything.

Learning that I need to stay in my personal business (Better Business Boundary) came with a difficult learning curve. I learned that it's okay to say no. There are times when it's downright necessary. Being in control of self includes not allowing other people to run us over in subtle and manipulative ways. We are in charge of how we allow others to treat us. Emotional manipulation may not be apparent at first, but it can drive us to say and do things we didn't intend. Not allowing negativity to take up residence within is important, because, otherwise, that which is beneficial can be subtracted, bringing about multiplied divisions. Maintaining a balanced and healthy life is partially dependent on setting and keeping healthy, clear, and definitive boundaries.

10/12/2020

As I look back on the child-rearing years and see the beautiful work God has created in each of our children, my heart overflows with joy. Our children taught me about the need for setting healthy boundaries. I learned that honesty, trust, fairness, and respect are key components of a healthy, balanced, and mutually agreeable relationship.

Spending time, thought, and energy on creating and maintaining healthy friendships is definitely worth it. Valued friendships are treasures that cannot be bought. They bring smiles to faces instead of frowns. True friends respect the boundaries of others. I am extremely grateful for every precious friend God has planted in my life to bring me joy and teach me hard truths through love. I value the opportunities to receive and reciprocate those blessings. "Every good gift and every perfect gift is from above, coming down from the Father of lights, with whom there is no variation or shadow due to change" (James 1:17 ESV).

11/9/2020

There is a continual process of clearing in life. Working through past pain is difficult, lengthy, and can be harrowing. Even when forgiveness has been given and prayers for blessings have been prayed, our enemy is on the prowl, seeking to kill, steal, and destroy our hearts, passion, dreams, creativity, and relationships. Succumbing to that reality in life will keep us hidden, silent, and ineffective for God's kingdom. We become stronger and equipped to, in Jesus' name, tell the enemy to back off when we realize what's really been going on behind the scenes.

Today, I was stuck in an emotionally heavy place. I chose to retreat to my art room, close the doors, open the window, feel the gentle breeze, and pray. In the quietness of the room, an unfinished project had been patiently waiting for these moments in time. As I worked on adding finishing touches to a handmade coffee table, I suddenly stopped. Looking around the room brought me comfort. Vinyl wall lettering had been chosen and perfectly centered on the wall by the previous homeowner. Five words from John Wooden's book *My Personal Best: Life Lessons from an All-American Journey* inspired me to keep going and be my best self, no matter what. "Make each day your masterpiece"[7] (John Wooden with Steve Jamison, *My Personal Best: Life Lessons from an All-American Journey* [McGraw Hill, 2004], 18.) was not just a quote on the wall; the five words spoke life into my soul. While I was working through my pain, God wanted me to be still, focus on Him, rest in His presence, count my blessings, and allow Him to calm my anxious spirit.

It came to my attention yesterday that talking about tough parts of my book in a deeper way had stirred up unhealed pain and unresolved issues for another person. I truly meant no harm, but I learned a wise tidbit worth sharing: get permission before opening up and dumping your load of stuff onto another person. Ask, "Do you have the capacity to receive any more into your personal space at this time?" Deep thinkers and sensitive people can benefit from this practice. It could help us avoid adding to someone else's pain and help us avoid setbacks in our own lives. Giving the potential recipient an opportunity to say, "Sorry, I can't handle any more right now," is a caring way to consider the interest of another. In caring for another person's interest in this way, we may also be protecting ourselves from additional injury.

This leads me back to how important it is to set healthy boundaries for ourselves. We aren't mind readers. For example, allowing a person to share tough things about their life gives the sharer a "go" signal that it's okay to continue, even though it is triggering to the receiver. The sharer may not realize the receiver inwardly wants them to stop until a time-out is called or the receiver leaves feeling wounded and offended, without saying anything.

Learning healthy communication skills is important to help us create healthy personal boundaries.

Inner healing doesn't happen on a schedule, and many days we take one step forward and two or more steps back. Working on healing is an important service we perform for ourselves. I call it "soul gardening" and "soul sprinkling." People will know when they've done enough work for one day. Loving others through their pain, even when their pain tears at our insides, is what we are called to do—no matter what, no matter when, no matter how long.

The seasons change, and we change and grow through the daily seasons of life. We are greeted with beauty and blessings every day. Purpose is waiting to be discovered. Life is not about us. We each have a story, and we each have a past. We can begin in the present to transform the ending of a life story. Positive changes produce positive results. Scripture helps us with these words: "We destroy arguments and every lofty opinion raised against the knowledge of God, and take every thought captive to obey Christ" (2 Corinthians 10:5 ESV).

Tested and tried human beings are like precious gemstones that have stood the test of time, encountered intense pressure, and endured extreme proverbial heat. Harold Simmons, a special man from a former church, shared this multifaceted insight: "[I must] prepare for the test before I am tested again. God will not give me the answers to my questions during the test."

Being unshakeable and unwavering describes individuals who are firm in their beliefs. The beliefs emerge in actions when we believe in something or someone beyond a shadow of a doubt. Our position and determination to stay the course no matter what are vital for us to glow, sparkle, and reflect God's light. My own resolve is a result of having followed through with setting better personal boundaries that are in alignment with God's will.

God's boundaries were created for our personal well-being, the betterment of interpersonal relationships, and making our relationships with Him the best they can be. Disappointments, unrealistic expectations of others, and opinions and judgment calls based only on what is visible from our perspectives can steer our thoughts into undesirable places and lead us to behave in unbecoming ways. When a door of opportunity opens, we have no way of knowing where that path will lead or what we will experience as a result. If this happens in a dark time, we may only know we long for relief instead of grief. I was in that place in August 2001.

A string of events had led me to a church where I was warmly welcomed by Shirley Meek Williams, and our friendship grew. She became the perfect confidential, compassionate, and nonjudgmental sounding board I needed to help me get through some troubling years. At the time, I was unaware that Shirley was a certified life coach with a master's degree in counseling. As the founder and owner of It's All About Change (which offers Christian life coaching for women), Shirley wants to "see clients stretch and grow beyond their wildest imagination."

God placed Shirley in my life to be a blessing in countless ways. I am so grateful. She helped me as I struggled with marital issues. However, that was not all. Shirley was my friend with a flashlight who walked beside me in my darkest years of being a mom. She knew what I was going through and held my hand so I wouldn't fall to pieces or lose sight of hope. Frightening things were taking place around me, and God knew I needed a prayerful and supportive friend who was also a trained counselor. God had me covered on all sides, inside and out. The emotional pain I was experiencing was further complicated when something I needed to face, and heal from, was rising up into awareness and would not let me go.

In 2006, during that particular season of pain, pyrography (woodburning) and relief carving became effective emotional outlets for me. I had been searching for creative ways to allow bottled-up and confusing emotions to flow out of me in constructive ways. Inner peace was a goal worth pursuing.

My first carved and woodburned "peace" plaque looked pitiful. I created a special design and burned it into the center of the plaque. After woodburning the word *PEACE* above it in capital letters, each letter looked huge compared to the smaller design below. The finished work silently screamed out the word I longed to feel. I kept playing around with the inexpensive beginner tools, then chose to purchase a professional woodburning set and quality carving knives in an effort to make the crafting sessions easier and more enjoyable.

During those disturbing days, I wanted to give a doctor the gift of a woodburned relief carving, because he had been so helpful to our family. When I asked what subject matter he preferred, he quickly said, "An armadillo."

"Okay! Is there a story behind the armadillo?"

The answer I received made sense. "Well, some doctors and I meet every week, and the armadillo is our mascot."

I didn't pry into the reasons why; I did my best to create an adorable armadillo (if an armadillo can look adorable). After all, it wasn't about the armadillo. The doctor was pleased with his new friend and proudly displayed his group's mascot on the fireplace mantel in his office. I photocopied the armadillo plaque, and it is on display in my art room. The experience makes me smile because I remember how good that gift made me feel as the giver—and in that time of pain, I was caring for myself in a special way through art.

11/16/2020

It was exciting to visit art studios and meet local artists yesterday. Heartfelt thanks go to Andrea Faye Boswell for establishing the Southern Hands Artist Studio Tour in 2013, bringing enjoyment to artists and guests for years to come (www.shastour.com). I look forward to the annual event the second weekend in November. Filled with awe and expectation, I woke up yesterday wondering which artists I would meet, which creative process I would learn, and what works of fine art would raise their proverbial hands and whisper, "Pick me! Pick me!"

A talented pyrographer's studio was first on my list. I was introduced to a Razertip® woodburning kit and multiple woodburning pens and tips. Manasi Joshi, the artist, offered to help steer me to her favorite pens and tips. I look forward to expanding my collection of useful and fun tools. Another treasure I discovered was a beautiful woodburned box ready to be personalized. Manasi said I could think about which words I might like for her to burn into the blank space on the lid. After much thought and reflection, I decided on five words: "Shine bright like a diamond!" Manasi had incorporated Swarovski crystals into some of her works on display. I also remembered my mom suggesting, "You need to include something sparkly in the things you make." Since the woodburned box represented me, it was fitting to have Manasi add a Swarovski crystal over the *i* in "diamond" to complete the outside of the box.

The inside of the box is being worked on by me. My plans are to add artistic details to the inside; embellishments will create interest when the box is opened. I'm not in any rush to make that happen. It will come in time. I have named this treasure my Think-and-Do Box. Even though the loose contents will change over time, the box has a name that well reflects its intended purpose. I have pondered over what it means to me to "shine bright like a diamond."

One way to keep shining is to take care of my health. A long-awaited treadmill will soon be delivered, and I look forward to becoming healthier physically through its use. In connection to that goal, the first item placed in the Think-and-Do Box was a bar of *very* dark chocolate. After each treadmill workout, I plan to give myself a bird's portion of the chocolate. Knowing that the yummy treat is waiting on me to "do" what I told myself I needed to "do" will help spur me into action. If I forget about the chocolate being there, it's perfectly okay.

Becoming healthier spiritually is also important since it allows God's light to shine from within. I've chosen to keep my mind, body, and spirit focused on God during my treadmill workouts and every waking hour. Spending time in prayer, meditation, and memorizing scripture verses are exciting ways to think about the treadmill's multiple purposes. In the privacy and quietness of our home, I will be daily walking and talking with Jesus, my best Friend. He will keep me on track with this word: "Come."

11/20/2020

Allowing the noise of emotions to get in the way of making sound decisions is counterproductive and can lead one to make rash decisions. Being intentional with forward thinking and considering new ideas requires us to pause, take a step back, and look at our lives from a broader perspective. It's hrad to wirte aoubt soemtihng we dno't konw in its fullenss, yet it's bneifiacil to exlproe waht hieds unedr the tip of the icerbeg. (Note: The typoglycemia in the previous sentence effectively makes the point.)

To satisfy my inquisitive mind, I need to learn how to have courageous conversations when necessary. Avoiding getting to the point of the matter is unhealthy and can make things worse. Our tendency to delay talking about something that's difficult or unpleasant can be partially based on fear of repercussions, consequences, or a lack of understanding about how to deal effectively with matters of concern.

Learning from the masters about any subject that matters to us and affects our relationships is worth the time, energy, expense, and dedication. I have discovered warmth, compassion, and wisdom can be found once we dare to undertake those difficult conversations. Sometimes all we need is a gentle arrow that points us to subjects we've never investigated before. We also must embrace the courage it takes to become better. Books and podcasts are helpful, and I appreciate those who share tips and wisdom with the world.

Sam Horn wrote an amazing book titled *Tongue Fu!®: How to Deflect, Disarm, and Defuse Any Verbal Conflict.*[8] I loaned the book out years ago, and it wasn't returned to my library. Jenni, a dear friend you will soon meet in the "Our Lady Cave" chapter of this book, knew I deeply missed that book and surprised me with a replacement. God laid that sincere act of love and kindness on Jenni's heart. Thank you, dear friend!

Masters in communication offer courses that can serve as rudders for relational ships that oftentimes veer off course. Skills learned can be utilized in everyday interactions to enrich communication in effective ways. Recognizing and admitting we need help in certain areas are the first steps to becoming willing and teachable participants as we are pruned, honed, and polished. Every individual can benefit on some level from the training that masters in communication offer. We can avoid and resolve many conflicts by working on the ways we listen, share, ask good questions, and love without judging.

Knowing what we need deep inside can be puzzling, but putting each life puzzle together with God's help is liberating. God gives us what we need when we need it and in ways we can understand. Aha moments become shaken loose when the proverbial two-by-four of awareness hits us between the eyes. It is then that our visions and God's purpose become clearer. The setting of essential boundaries is often prompted by a series of mishaps. There is purpose in the pain, and we need to thank God for it all. "There is an appointed time for everything. And there is a time for every matter under heaven" (Ecclesiastes 3:1 NASB).

Sharon Jaynes wrote a book titled *When You Don't Like Your Story: What If Your Worst Chapters Could Become Your Greatest Victories?* It offers an insightful perspective on suffering. She invites us to think deeply with these words: "Rather than view the pain as our burden to bear, what if we considered it a gift for growing? Healing on the other side of heartbreak is not simply returning to how we were before the rending, but becoming better than we would have been without it—someone stronger, someone wiser, someone gentler."[9]

It's about Time:
BOTSOTBE

"And whatever you do or say, do it as a representative of the Lord Jesus, giving thanks through Him to God the Father."

—Colossians 3:17 NLT

6/8/2009

A bad habit has worked its way into my life, and I have taken the initiative to kick it out. A commitment to be on time is an excellent way to help myself be not only prompt but early. Developing new ways of thinking and embedding them into my brain will enable me to create new paths for character development. It's about time.

I've realized that when I'm not on time, I am not considering the interests of others. Selfishness offends God and other people and can make one feel bad about oneself. As I choose to grow up in all areas, being on time will help in the development process. Changing my thinking and retraining my mind will take work, but it will be worth all the time it might take to help me become more productive and use my time wisely.

Setting the clocks ahead of time was meant to scare me into hurrying up, but those efforts to trick my brain didn't work. I did the math. My brain knew better, and so did I. My focus, instead, will be on appropriate activities that will ensure a habitude of promptitude, which will emerge from a correct attitude.

Attitudes can be positive, negative, or neutral. If one has a neutral attitude, problems often are ignored and one becomes complacent with the way things are. To manage my time well, I must go through the days with a positive mindset. Otherwise, I'll naturally revert to the way things were in the past. Allowing time for emergencies, traffic, and other surprises will be a useful part of this strategy and new way of thinking.

Bad habits can be broken, and good habits can be developed and serve as reinforcements. A person's heart and attitude will be displayed publicly through the things they say and do. My tardiness showed my need for an attitude adjustment. Getting my priorities in order and doing what was right required me to focus on loving and pleasing God first. Being a good steward of the gift of time will show others that I care about them and recognize their time is valuable also. The following entry gives an account of how my particular *garden of time* grew.

I enjoyed getting ready for church yesterday. It was a beautiful Sunday morning, and all was well within. Gary left for church early, and I found myself in "Brenda World." Since I had given myself plenty of time to get ready, there was no need to rush. Peaceful music was playing, a fresh cup of coffee was beside me, and an aromatherapy candle had been lit. The area had been perfectly staged for me to put on my makeup. I enjoy having my space and time to be alone. Many days, this space includes a pen and paper to record thoughts before they become lost forever. This morning was no exception.

The time I had been trying so hard to keep up with suddenly flew by and got ahead of me. I was late to church—again. I walked through the parking lot, wondering how all the other people (represented by their empty cars) could get to church on time. I silently asked myself, "Why is this such a struggle for me?" Feeling frustrated and disappointed in myself, I apologized to the first person I saw in the hall. Along with the apology came these words: "One day, I will be here five minutes before the service begins."

One day was my goal and intent as I asked the special lady in the hall how she did it. Even though the first service was now underway, she had arrived already for the second service. That way, she explained, she would be in place for whatever God might have in store for her. In talking with her further, I came to understand there may be people in the halls who need a hug, smile, encouraging word, or sympathetic ear before church begins. If I'm not where I should be at my God-appointed post (whenever or wherever that might be), I'm not available for God to use me.

This earth angel named Melodye added, "I am the same way at work and everywhere else I go." She had been given a fitting name at birth. God planted Melodye in the hall that morning to reach out and touch my heart with wise and helpful, harmonious words. I was shown a living example that led me in the right direction. Being early is like going the second mile before beginning the first.

God spoke to my heart during the church service, and I penned these words: "When I make up my mind to do something, I'm there 100 percent. Today, I made a commitment to be accountable to God alone so that I would keep up with the Earth's clock and be fashionably early. It's all about commitment and respect. I choose this day (June 7, 2009) to be a new beginning in my life, marked by a dedication to being on time." The visiting pastor from Kenya shared in his message that we can move forward with confidence because the eye of the Lord is always on us. He will meet our needs at the right time.

I cannot teach what I don't live out on a daily basis. Responding to others in the way I would like them to respond to me helps my life run smoother. Being on time is *being ready and in my seat when the bell rings*. If I'm not five minutes early, then I need to consider myself late. God is always on time. Knowing that I am human and that things will come up that may alter plans, I have chosen to strive to BOT (be on time), SOT (stay on task), and BE (be early). Being on time is a thoughtful way to "do what leads to peace and to mutual edification" (Romans 14:19). It can help reduce conflicts and boosts self-esteem. The acronym BOTSOTBE is symbolic of new beginnings. An energetic and positive mindset is a great place to begin.

I have bathed in prayer my intentions to ingrain this habit into my life. Philippians 4:13 (NKJV) tells me, "I can do all things through Christ who strengthens me." It is through our weaknesses that God makes us strong.

2/22/2021

During the season of creating new pathways of thought regarding time, I carried a small alarm clock with me. The actual alarm wasn't used, but I glanced at the clock's face many times while getting ready for appointments. The letters BOTSOTBE adhered to the clock became a constant reminder and kept me on guard against anything that could distract me. It was a vital tool to keep time from passing without notice.

I used a twenty-one-day plan to reprogram my mind, and I created a spreadsheet using pen and paper. A space was left where a smiley face could be added when I was on time or early. There were only three days during the twenty-one-day period when I missed the mark. For those three days, I still gave myself a smiley face instead of a frowny one. Trying was not failing; it was giving the day my best effort.

Over the years, I've gotten better and better at being on time and staying on task, and I enjoy the refreshing feeling that comes with being early. Working hard on this habit that truly matters has been—and will always be—time well spent.

A TIME FOR THOUGHT

When Earth and time have passed away and humans are no more,
There won't be forests, stones, or springs, no bios or folklore.
Our penned life songs will mark their times; pasts will be brought to light.
We'll give account for good and bad, no time for fight or flight.

Back in the times of Noah when the ark's door was closed tight,
The eight who chose to obey were kept safe. God's way proved right.
God formed in us the right to choose; each has their own free will.
Who will we choose? How will we live? We're not robots of steel.

When time stands still, 'twill be too late to choose to love God's Son.
The King of kings and Lord of lords is God, the Three-in-One.
God gives us many chances, yet our time to choose will end.
I'd rather bow to Christ on Earth before "The End" begins.

Brenda Eller
7/13/2010

"Do not let your hearts be troubled. You believe in God, believe
also in me."

—John 14:1

Getting Ohgeenized

"Outer disorder and clutter creates (or may indicate) inner turmoil and chaos. In contrast, uncluttered spaces in home and office bring a sense of peace and stimulate creativity."[10]

—Sue Augustine

8/4/2016

Cleaning up my physical environment included sorting out, organizing, tidying up, and removing anything that wasn't beneficial to my mind, heart, spirit, body, home, yard, or relationships. Anything (people were included) that interfered with my relationship with God and others was on the list to be *ohgeenized* and put in its proper place.

1/23/2018

Special treasures awaited me as I sifted through boxes and bags filled with art and schoolwork from our children's growing-up years. Since I didn't know what to save and what to discard, I saved most of their work. Catching a glimpse into the heart of Jeff when he was in tenth grade brought tears to my eyes. A science observation project captured my attention. Over a period of four months, Jeff had documented his observations of temperature, settings, soil, animals, changes in food sources, rainfall, organisms, and the emergence of plants along with some personal thoughts from him.

At the end of the comments section, Jeff shared his heart with the teacher on June 6, 1996. I share his heartfelt words with permission: "I feel tired and worn out to the bone. As I was sitting at the tree observing, my thoughts wandered to summertime. Not a whole lot of time will be there either. I know I chose my time, but just sitting in the woods or watching a bird's nest or bumming around in the creek (examples) just don't come every day. Sometimes I wish I was little again. I want to unwind and crash in the woods. I want to lie on the grass and watch the clouds. I want to breathe the fresh air of summertime and the forest. I want to go fishing at 5:00 a.m. I want to go backpacking through the Appalachians, Smokies, Cohuttas, and Blue Ridge Mountains. These are the riches of a world that depends so often on pictures. I want to see, experience, and hear things more than look at pictures. I want to be free."

Somebody else might have turned away from the boxes and bags in the basement—with their memories of hard yet joy-filled years—and thrown them away. But I didn't, couldn't, and wouldn't. Those years and the lives being lived were of great importance to me because those lives were—and are—a huge part of mine.

Our daughter Erin learned about the word *organize* as a toddler. She pronounced it in an adorable way: "ohgeenize." I chose to keep her pronunciation alive.

As our children were growing up, it became necessary to help them clean their rooms. It would have been easier on me to let them keep the doors closed, but that wouldn't have taught them important tidying-up techniques.

Kristyn still remembers the creative way her toy hoop was used as a teaching tool. When she was young and her bedroom was messy, I placed the toy on the floor, filled the circular boundary with items for her to put away, set the timer, then did it again multiple times until her room was tidy. The process helped her learn to focus on the tiny mess in the circle instead of feeling overwhelmed by the disorder as a whole. It was exhausting for both of us, but the end result was satisfying. Helping our children clean their rooms seemed to be a constant struggle. I understand how they must have felt with that dreaded and daunting task continually before them.

3/11/2011

Tedious tasks can trouble and tire the most tenacious of people when the tasks that speak the loudest are telling us uncomfortable truths. I have procrastinated long enough, yet I'm finding it difficult to begin the lengthy and grueling process of clearing our home of what needs to be put in its place or laid to rest.

Effective solutions don't have to be perfect. The real issue is not the papers but the person who placed the papers in the boxes and bags. Tucking papers away to take care of later allows them time to accumulate. (In the case of this book, the extra time turned out to be a good thing.)

The following are important words of advice from stroke victim Mary Alice Odom. "Please . . . don't put off until tomorrow what you can do today because nobody can know what each tomorrow holds."

4/23/2013

Determination, perseverance, a positive attitude, and the will to succeed will bring about one success after another. I am the one who needs to sort through the boxes and bags because my heart is deeply invested. Important papers are in the jumbled jungle somewhere, like my parents' wills.

While life was happening around me and to me, putting out the hottest fires was the best I could do given the challenging and complicated set of circumstances. However, the need to organize had become a hot fire I couldn't ignore any longer. The time was nigh. Ingenuity, creativity, and I needed to get to work. The plan of action needed to be gentle, simple, validating, and loving.

With no commitments on the calendar for today, I had a perfect opportunity to ohgeenize "the Room" and clean up the mess I myself had made. The small bedroom served as my office, a place of rest, and the gathering room for papers that didn't have a pre-set place to go. In addition, it was where the raw material for this book was being stored. Cramming papers and things in boxes, bags, closets, and drawers is not a good filing system.

Through the years, I've wasted valuable time and energy because I believed I lacked the time and space to put things in order. The truth is that I didn't have the energy to face the reality of what was occurring in my life, slowly rising up to be revealed. Sue Augustine's words described my situation well: "Outer disorder and clutter creates (or may indicate) inner turmoil and chaos." Decluttering would bring about a "sense of peace and stimulate creativity."

I am at a pivotal place in my life where I can make use of those things that money cannot buy. The gifts of time, space, reflection, experience, and an acceptance of reality are helping breathe life into dark places and helping transform chaos into order.

My half-hearted attempts to ohgeenize had not worked in the past. I awoke today willing to approach this beast from a different angle. Sneaking up on the mess was a game I was eager to play, squaring off against the part of myself that had resisted this task in the past. With my choice to declutter, creativity had already been stimulated! This is how I played the game, making up the rules as I went:

1. Strip the bed and wash linens. Put pillows, blankets, and bedspread in another room until the work is done.

2. Eat breakfast, talk to a friend on the phone, drink coffee, write the chapter "Toxicity to Tonicity" for this book, put sheets in the dryer, and eat a snack.

3. Light candles, turn on peaceful music, prepare a second cup of coffee, remove the bedroom door from its hinges, and set it aside. (The messy room was now exposed, and the bedroom door couldn't be shut. Keeping the door closed had been my way of hiding the mess. When the door was removed, a point was made that my motives were sincere. I committed myself to do what it took to accomplish this mission.)

4. Put on my favorite shirt that Gary likes so that when he comes home from work, he might not notice the mess.

5. Approach the beast from a different angle. Work from the ceiling down, beginning with cleaning the dusty ceiling fan.

6. Clean the blinds and wall decor. (The mess still doesn't know about my plans. And I am still not sure about the details. All I know is I'm

doing something constructive in "the Room" and feeling proud of myself for beginning the process. Being determined to set myself free from any prison cell of my own making is worth the thought, time, and effort it might take.)

7. Done. I have not yet tackled the files (aka piles) on the floor, but I was successful in cleaning all other parts of the room. That makes me feel better about myself and hopeful that the job can be completed by nightfall or, at the latest, bedtime.

8. Eight is the number for new beginnings, a fresh start. Gently place small piles of unrelated items on the mattress. Patiently go through them one by one.

9. Dinner with Gary.

10. Bedtime. I did not complete the task, but that is okay. After all, it took a while for the room to get in its current state. With the room clean, the outlook is brighter. I feel encouraged and empowered. Small successes work wonders. Devoting time, love, care, and attention to this area of my life has turned the beast into a blast!

11. My new rule is to *stop* adding to the pile. If something sits around for more than twenty-five days in our home in a place it shouldn't be, I have a plan in place to do something about it. I liken the accumulation of stuff to the way that debt accrues. Most charge-card companies give customers a grace period of about twenty-five days to pay the bill in full with no interest charges. My plan of attack will free up precious time for the things that truly matter. Papers can accumulate the same way that debt can, so remember to put papers and things in their proper places. I will now carefully consider each item before bringing it into our home. If something was given or sent to me, I will do something with it in a timely manner—store it in a proper place, give it away, recycle it, discard it, or shred it. The plan will work if I stick to it and remain resolute in keeping these healthy personal commitments.

Creating an impressive end to unimpressive beginnings showed me there are countless wandering paths in life that eventually come full circle. Understanding

how a problem began is the key to preventing future messes and disturbing situations. Since I began documenting my life and putting experiences, thoughts,
and feelings onto paper, I've become armed with knowledge I didn't have when
some important parts of life would slip by without notice. Being unarmed
and vulnerable left me open to severe hardships. Before I took up the habit
of putting words to paper, I was often overwhelmed, distracted, and bogged
down by all the craziness that had occurred through the years.

Slowly but surely, my tendencies to procrastinate were met with an expanse
of time I dedicated to the task at hand in the case of "the Room." Overthinking
could no longer keep me from doing what needed to be done. Procrastination
had its payday and found this gal learning valuable lessons that will last
a lifetime.

GROWING, GROWING, GONE!

4/23/2013

I've slept near this beast a bit.
Today, I'm thinking well of it.
Pretending it was debt I owed,
I saw how piles had slowly grown.

My diligence will soon pay off.
The interest earned helped thoughts turn soft.
This systematic plan will work;
Life plans are filled with countless "firsts."

Now, don't you think it's rather odd
That I removed the door? Yes, nod.
Drastic, perhaps, yet truth be told,
I must be done with what's grown old.

Sometimes what's old is seen anew—
A treasure, not a beast that grew.
Start at the top to clean room best;
It clears the mind to do the rest.

Comparing this task to real life
Is helpful when it comes to strife.
When we don't deal with what can hurt,
It looks like trash. We feel like dirt.

We shut that door then lock it tight.
The key's secure, kept out of sight.
We dare not let one person in
'Cause they may frown instead of grin.

When we get tired, have "had enough,"
It's time to deal with our old stuff.
Take courage, then. Let someone see.
I pray you're treated graciously.

I chose success. The plan won't fail.
"The Room"? It had a tale to tell.
The piles? I'll work on and not hide.
The door's now hung; it's opened wide.

BASK IN THE TASK

A task is what one makes it, depending on their view.
Heavy thoughts can make a task difficult to do.
Unpleasantness and dread will steal each blessing that awaits.
The task at hand could turn to joy if one anticipates.

Visualize in the mind a task already done.
It'll help to make the best of it. The task could be great fun.
Enjoyment in the hardest things is possible, it's true.
So, think of blessings in this way: "It's what I get to do!"

I'm thankful for two eyes that see each task in front of me.
Two arms hold hands that can still work. Two legs stand on two feet.
I choose to thank God for the help He graciously gives me.
Deriving pleasure from hard tasks, I'll bask in them with glee.

Brenda Eller
7/26/2009

DIG Pest Control

It is in times of grief and distress that we can often get a better grasp on the inner struggles we have long wrestled with. Taking a pen and pad to a secluded area, writing feelings down as they come, and capturing them in their rawness and transparency can help us examine our fears and pain in enlightening and refreshing ways. Transformations in our lives can miraculously begin when we change the way we think about *what is* instead of focusing and dwelling on *what was* which still brings us pain.

Facing our fears and hurts and inspecting them, as if they are enclosed in clear lidded jars, can help us give them names. By asking ourselves, "What is the worst thing that can happen?" and answering the question honestly, we can summon up the courage to take a closer look without self-defensiveness and self-preservation obscuring our view. By picking up the figurative clear jars with the freshly captured specimens, we are able to look at all sides of those things we have allowed to capture and poison our souls, and we can do so without feeling attacked or being harmed.

On April 27, 2014, a large, scary-looking black spider was on our driveway, crawling toward our garage door. I can handle granddaddy longlegs, but this spider made me feel unsettled. It wasn't hurting anyone, and I didn't want to harm it, but I didn't want to find it later in our home. I made a mad dash to the basement to retrieve an empty mayonnaise jar I had known would come in handy one day. With the clear jar on the driveway and its mouth facing the approaching spider, I watched as the creature walked into the jar without realizing what was happening.

I let my curiosity out long enough to explore the spider's behavior after my heart had stopped racing. With a lid on the jar, I felt protected. The spider remained still until I opened the lid and did something that made the occupant of the jar feel threatened. Although the small stick I was holding barely touched the spider, the creature instantly went into attack mode.

That's how people behave! We can be having a great day, not hurting a flea, and then someone will say or do something that instantly sets off explosives within. Sadly, we let the memories of those moments linger long after we feel the touch of those prickly sticks.

After the experiment was over and my curiosity had been satisfied, I laid the opened jar on its side with its mouth facing the woods, not me. The spider slowly walked away. I felt good about letting it go for a walk in the woods on its own, unharmed. We all know what would have happened if I had left the spider in the jar, closed the lid and left it alone. Over time, the spider would have died. That would not have been my intent or desire.

The spider taught me life lessons worth keeping alive forever. When we let scary and painful things remain lodged in our souls instead of facing them and letting them go, we are wasting our time, energy, and resources by tending to unhealthy gardens that don't produce good fruits. People tend to go into attack mode when they feel threatened or when some inner hurt is triggered. This natural reflex is common to men, women, boys, and girls.

Any thoughts of crushing and killing the spirit of a human being must be squelched instead of going unacknowledged and unaddressed. Each individual is responsible for working with God on their own heart wounds. The longer we hold onto our pain, the worse the pain will be. Until we make the choice to forgive ourselves, forgive others, let it out, and let it go, we keep ourselves enclosed in a jar called captivity. We may think nobody can see inside the dark jars we find ourselves in from time to time, yet God can clearly see our hearts. When we realize we're stuck, the fantastic gift of awareness offers us the opportunity to make choices that help our gardens in life produce good fruit.

When we ignorantly become focused on negative emotions, we remain paralyzed and stuck in the web called fear. That's where doubt resides. Becoming able to see and name our fears helps us better understand why we feel the way we do. Remaining calm amid chaos is a skill I chose to adopt, but it's easier said than done. Being a first responder to my heart and mind means I will always be getting lessons in prayer, practices, perception, and patience.

Our family was clearing out my great-aunt's house shortly before her death, and I found an eleven-page *Guideposts Magazine* booklet from 1974. On the cover was a photo of Norman Vincent Peale. His mini-message titled "What to Do When Things Upset You"[11] was appropriate and caught my attention. The main point was repeated several times and became a magnet for my heart and mind. Words in Isaiah 26:3 (KJV) continue to be a lighthouse for my soul's well-being: "Thou wilt keep him in perfect peace whose mind is stayed on thee."

I chose to dig for deeper meaning in that verse, and The Amplified Bible, Classic Edition (AMPC) magnified it this way: "You will guard him and keep him in perfect and constant peace whose mind (both its inclination and its character) is stayed on You, because he commits himself to You, leans on You, and hopes confidently in You." These undeniable truths are real and help me to remain focused on my faith in God's provision, protection, and preservation of my soul. I've earnestly prayed for peace time and time again. God keeps teaching me through hard lessons what He wants me to learn and never forget: "Thou wilt keep him in perfect peace whose mind is stayed on thee" (KJV).

As a result of putting problems onto paper, I was able to process feelings of entrapment that were outgrowths of unhealthy coping mechanisms. If I don't stay vigilant, this lack of preparedness could be a "present" I get to reopen every day in the future. Giving in to fears and insecurities will keep them hanging around. They won't go away on their own. I must let them go. Releasing them by name one at a time will help set me free from whatever is troubling my spirit. The enemy enjoys watching our composure crumble. Asking God to come and roll the stone away (the lid to whatever tomb I might find myself in) gives me the courage to let the scary spiders in my life go for a nice walk in the woods—away from my heart and home.

It's refreshing when we let the spiders in our lives become highly regarded friends instead of perceiving them as enemies. We take our power back when

we can thank our personal pests for giving us insights into our inner worlds—
then choose to let the scary things go.

Keep digging and exploring. They are good things. DIG—do it generously!

Choice: Hide or Abide?

JANUARY 2010

"The Lord is my light and my salvation; whom shall I fear? The Lord is the defense of my life; whom shall I dread?"

— Psalm 27:1 NASB 1995

"I would have despaired unless I had believed that I would see the goodness of the Lord in the land of the living. Wait for the Lord; be strong and let your heart take courage; yes, wait for the Lord."

—Psalm 27:13–14 NASB 1995

For many months, I've been torn about whether to include in the book the most profound experience of my life. The event has affected my life in ways I couldn't have foreseen at the time. I've struggled with not knowing what repercussions the truth might have on the hearts of others. But how could I possibly write a book about how my gardens grew and leave out the most heartbreaking and difficult-to-fathom chapter of my life? A verse from Proverbs has been planted in my mind and heart for guidance: "Fear of man will prove to be a snare, but whoever trusts in the Lord is kept safe" (29:25).

An unanswered question that kept me stuck for years was "What would people think of me if they only knew?" My choice to remain silent was exactly what Satan wanted all along. I fell for his lies and tricks, which kept me bound tightly in his grip. After all, "the thief comes only to steal and kill and destroy" (John 10:10). I kept family, close friends, and acquaintances in the dark because I feared their condemnation, lack of compassion, and the general absence of unconditional love for me as a fellow human being.

Although I am always mindful of not hurting others with the things I choose to share, I feel other troubled souls could find some peace in the healing wisdom God placed on my heart when I faced my painful truths at last. My purpose in sharing this long-held secret is not to bring up pain in the lives of others. Instead, I do so with the knowledge that God will never allow our painful life experiences to be unusable unless we make the unwise choice to dig our own holes, bury our ugly pasts, and do our best to forget about the bad. Too often, that is what we do, thinking what's done has been done and we cannot change it.

I have sought wise counsel and received advice from trusted confidantes, hearing everything from "You have to put it in the book" to "It would hurt too many" to "That's a tough one. I don't know." Still torn, I chose to earnestly seek God's specific word to me on the matter since He is the Mighty Counselor and Prince of Peace.

Within minutes of my earnest prayer for wisdom, I thought of the small book I kept handy titled *God's Words of Life From the NIV Women's Devotional Bible.* It has comforted me on countless occasions. In the "Devotional Thought on Guidance" by Marjorie Holmes, I found the perfect words for this time of true need. God used them to help soothe my unsettled heart.

Everybody should have a friend like Ralph. He can fix a lamp or a lawn mower, refinish furniture, build bookshelves. All by himself he has transformed his garage into a workshop and completely remodeled his mother's house.

One day, marveling at these results over coffee, I asked, "Ralph, where did you learn to do all this?" Thoughtfully he sipped his coffee, his blue eyes twinkling.

Then Ralph gave me the words of his own special prayer:

> *Jesus stand beside me.*
> *Guide and direct my life.*
> *Teach me what I need to know.*
> *Help me with my work.*
> *Let me serve you and others,*
> *That I may be worthy of God's grace.*

Ralph's special prayer has become a part of my own life now. I say it every morning. And all day. Whenever I am anxious or confused about a situation, one phrase comes to my rescue: "Teach me what I need to know." Of all the things Ralph has done to help me, his prayer has helped most of all.[12]

I in turn have allowed this special prayer to become a part of my own life now, and I pass it on as Marjorie Holmes has so eloquently done. Creating an acronym using the first letters of each line in Ralph's prayer (JGTHLT) helps me remember his heartfelt request of God. JGTHLT to me means "just go to Him like this." As I share my heart in the story that will follow, Jesus is standing beside me and will continue to be with me as I abide in Him.

"Commit everything you do to the LORD. Trust in him, and he will help you" (Psalm 37:5 NLT).

The next chapter, written in a memorandum format, describes a part of my life I'd hidden, one that had baffled me for years. Memos contain matter that is directive, advisory, and informative; the following memorandum is no exception. It is extremely personal and bares the innermost part of my soul. As I risk much by sharing much, I believe and trust that my healing journey will be helpful, even life changing, for many who are hurting or tormented.

"The sacrifices of God are a broken spirit; a broken and a contrite heart, God, You will not despise" (Psalm 51:17 NASB).

"Memo: Not Random" is a fitting title for the next chapter and its contents. The words were divinely inspired at 4:02 a.m. on February 2, 2010—almost one year after this particular healing process began (February 3, 2009). The time I will describe has made a distinctive mark in the thread of my life experiences. And I can see the hands of God working, shaping, and forming me for His glory and good purposes in spite of my grave errors in judgment and mistakes. I'm still under construction and am grateful that God isn't finished with me yet.

Devin Brewington and I attended church together, and words from his heart softly echo today: "Your biggest secret can turn into your biggest testimony."

Memo: Not Random

TO: Whom This Concerns
FROM: My Heart to Yours
DATE: February 2, 2010, 4:02 a.m.

On my sixth birthday, I received a white leather Bible from my grandparents. It has a zipper around the leather to protect the gold-tipped pages. It is the Bible I used in Bible drills when I was growing up and the one I read at home as a child. Dressed up in my frilly dresses with itchy petticoats underneath, I attended church every Sunday because my parents wouldn't have it any other way.

I vividly remember one particular Sunday morning when I carried my white leather Bible to church. My look was complete with crooked, freshly cut bangs and polished black patent-leather shoes. While I was sitting in the gray fold-up chair in the Sunday school room, my teacher wrote a scripture verse on the chalkboard that has impacted my life through the years. I wrote the verse in the front of that Bible for quick review. It reads, "Study to shew thyself approved unto God, a workman that needeth not to be ashamed, rightly dividing the word of truth" (2 Timothy 2:15 KJV). This particular verse became like an invisible necklace I wore around my neck. The verse served as a reminder to obey God and to do my best not to disappoint or hurt my parents.

At the age of nine, as I was listening to a sermon from the back row in church, I felt a tug on my heart that grew stronger and stronger. I knew it was God calling me to ask Jesus into my heart, which I did on that day. Knowing that I had chosen eternal life with my heavenly Daddy comforted me as a nine-year-old insecure and shy redhead. Even though I didn't fully understand the concept at the time, all human beings are born into sin. Even the most righteous and good people are in need of God's love, grace, mercy, and forgiveness, because Romans 3:23 tells us, "All have sinned and fall short of the glory of God." I had read, heard, and believed John 3:16, which is still one of my favorite scriptures: "For God so loved the world that He gave His only begotten Son, that whoever believes in Him should not perish but have everlasting life" (NKJV). At the young age of nine, I understood the words that Jesus spoke to Thomas and to humankind: "I am the way, and the truth, and the life; no one comes to the Father except through Me" (John 14:6 NASB).

Seven years later, on the evening of July 25, 1972, the youth choir at church presented a musical called *Purpose: A Contemporary Musical for Youth* by J. Phillip Landgrave.[13] After we had practiced the musical multiple times, the lyrics began to saturate my soul and penetrate my heart. During our performance, I sang about the need to ask God to bother my spirit when He knew I was heading in the wrong direction or doing anything that caused Him grief. I also learned that my purpose is only found in Christ. While I was singing in front of the church that Sunday in July, God spoke directly to my heart in a mighty way. The culprits of fear and doubt had been creeping into my heart and made me question the decision I'd made that Sunday morning when I was nine years old and accepted Christ. That age-old destructive duo had won out over the age-old dynamic duo called faith and belief. Wanting to be certain that I had truly received Jesus into my heart when I was nine, I rededicated my life to following Him.

As I grew older, there were times I selfishly made choices that didn't match up with God's desires. My people-pleasing tendencies didn't serve me well. To develop and grow into the person God meant for me to be, I learned the hard way that I needed to be pliable and humble, willing to be rebuked, corrected, trained, and disciplined.

Having been raised in a loving Christian home since birth, I was taught truths that were based on Jesus' teachings, along with the best ways to live and be. Even though I was being taught and trained from the best instruction book of all time, knowing what is in the Bible and applying those lessons to everyday life were sometimes two different things for me. I knew the difference between right and wrong, and applying God's truth to my life was easy when I was around friends from the youth group at church.

Feeling loved, accepted, and validated was very important to me, an insecure gal who had the thrill of being named to the homecoming court during the fall quarter of tenth grade. Surrounded by amazing and cherished friends, both on and off the drill team, I succumbed to internal and external pressures to fit in with the crowd at school, during social time, and around town. Friends, instead of God, became my focus during my junior and senior years in high school. Friendships blossomed, and I blossomed. Yet I no longer allowed my real first love, Jesus Christ, to have first place in my life. My self-esteem got a further boost when I was one of three senior girls chosen to be on the homecoming court. Even though I wasn't crowned homecoming queen, it was a huge honor to be on the football field in an evening gown, surrounded by my friends from the drill team. I felt like I was in my prime, and life felt exceptionally good.

After two final elective courses of guitar and chorus, I had enough credits to graduate early in March of 1974. While my former classmates were busy working to complete their last semester, I was blessed with a full-time job. I enjoyed working at a department store and meeting new people there. In my free time, I loved playing tennis with my best friend, who had also graduated early. Feeling grown-up and mature, I appreciated my newfound freedom as I waited for my freshman year of college to begin.

I met a guy during my early teenage years, and our paths crossed again in the summer of 1974. When his smooth words and captivating charm reeled me in, I became hooked on flattery. The words he used made me feel beautiful and desirable. After meeting up and hanging out several times, our time together ended in a startling way.

In the summer shortly after my eighteenth birthday, I discovered I was pregnant. Shock filled me to the core, uncertainty raced in to ramp up my anxiety, and fear paralyzed me as I considered the multitude of ways things could play out over the coming days, weeks, months, and years. I was frightened and unable to move forward, not knowing what to do.

My parents had always been hush-hush when it came to matters of sexuality, and I knew better than to approach them with news of this unintended pregnancy. Fear of their reaction quickly stopped me from any further consideration of seeking guidance from them. In my ignorant, desperate, and panic-stricken state of being, I felt lost, helpless, and alone. I had no one to confide in except for a few friends. *Now, what do I do?* was the question on my mind every waking hour. As I weighed my choices, time was running out to make my decision.

I had a fleeting thought about running away to have the baby and giving it up for adoption, but I wouldn't have been able to keep the pregnancy hidden from my parents. As I mentioned at the beginning of this chapter, I never wanted to do anything that would disappoint or hurt them. I was scared of the fallout that would have likely come between us. Courage and bravery were foreign to me at the time. And besides that, where would I have gone? There was no internet then. I only had the Yellow Pages business directory and a rotary phone. I didn't know where to turn or what to do. Where could I hide? What would I tell people? Who would help me pay for expenses? I certainly didn't have any money!

Even if I had chosen to have the child, our risky and foolish actions would have placed an enormous financial burden, emotional strain, and physical responsibility on my parents, who were not prepared to manage such an upheaval in their lives. I couldn't do that to them. The eighteen-year-old sperm donor believed abortion to be the best option, and he bowed out of all responsibility. His attitude and unwillingness to bear responsibility and be supportive did not surprise me at all. (Important note to those who knew me at the time: the donor was *not* my ex-fiancé.)

I felt lost and all alone; it was just me and my tumor. That is what the pregnancy truly felt like. Since I had recently turned eighteen, I was old enough to exercise my legal right to have an abortion without my parents' knowledge. *Roe v. Wade* seemed to have come to my rescue just in time, with abortion having just become legal one year and eight months before the time came for me to make my decision.

Abortion was the only option I believed I had. My selfishness and the selfishness of the donor had kept us from seriously considering the consequences of our unrestrained thoughts and actions. In giving in to momentary wants with the wrong person at the wrong time in my life, I had misused the gift God created to be enjoyed within the confines of marriage.

The counselor at the abortion clinic told me "it" was "just a blob of tissue" at the time of my procedure. Her words made me feel better about my decision to bring this crisis to an end. Afterward, I pushed the whole experience as far away from my thoughts as possible. It was the only way I could cope. Choosing to keep my secret buried for years was a coping mechanism to protect myself. However, the night Gary proposed, I shared it with him because I believed he had a right to know. After hearing that confession, he still loved me and wanted to marry me. Fear has many faces, and I have learned an important fact about fear: "The fear of the LORD is a fountain of life, turning a person from the snares of death" (Proverbs 14:27).

How could something that was once so important to me in my Christian walk be compromised as greatly as my values were back then? What happened to that verse I had chosen years ago to "hang around my neck"? I had made the choice to totally leave God out of my decision-making process. I had, in fact, made no choice at all, acting without thinking. And that, in reality, is a choice in and of itself. Hindsight teaches me that if I had set firm and healthy boundaries for myself, they would have protected me from a crisis pregnancy and the resulting tragedy. A decision to say no before temptation comes can sound an alarm in the mind of one who truly desires to remain pure and chaste for their future mate.

In retrospect, setting personal goals and placing great value on my worth, integrity, and destiny would have been the wisest choices for me to make on a daily basis. Guarding my heart and mind beforehand would have given me a means of escape before I became swept away by God-given, healthy, and normal emotions. It wasn't until years later that I understood the unwanted "tumor" I had seen as malignantly growing inside me had really been my first child. That's how far I'd pushed the experience out of my mind; that reality would have been too hard to face.

As a woman who has gone through an abortion, I have felt the need to hide the experience and pain from a world that is often quick to judge. Every day of my adult life, I have unconsciously been coping with the abortion through a variety of avoidance techniques. In an effort to protect myself from additional emotional harm, I unconsciously adjusted my behavior as I tried to be the best mom I could to our three children. Even though I didn't realize it as they were growing up, I tried hard not to let them see me fail at anything. It was important to me to set the best example I could during their impressionable years and afterward. Unbeknownst to me, this was, in fact, unhealthy because it is important for our children of all ages to know that parents are human beings just like them and that we make mistakes from time to time just as they do.

It wasn't until the reality of the abortion resurfaced and stared me down that I learned of a form of post-traumatic stress disorder called post-abortion syndrome. In 2008, when I began examining my life and recording thoughts through writing, I was also reading books by various authors. One of the books was a gift from our dear friends Merry and Dave Boehi. Two of their friends, Barbara Rainey and Susan Yates, wrote a book titled *Barbara & Susan's Guide to the Empty Nest: Discovering New Purpose, Passion & Your Next Great Adventure.* It was in their subsection called "Reflect on the Past with Courage" that I discovered the true source of my inner turmoil and distress. I read about a special lady named Pat who reflected on her past with courage instead of fear. Pat shared her abortion story and how it had negatively impacted many aspects of her life and relationships, even her relationship with God. Pat now helps other women who have had abortions find hope, courage, and healing.[14]

During my healing journey, I felt compelled to do further research on post-abortion syndrome. I had to find out why I had overreacted so intensely when negative stimuli from later traumas triggered me to freak out with our youngest child during her teenage years. Barbara Rainey and Susan Yates shared an important tool as a recommended resource for women who have gone through abortions. That tool is a book written by an amazing woman, Sydna Massé. Each word that she wrote made perfect sense. I reached out to Sydna after reading the book, *Her Choice to Heal: Finding Spiritual and Emotional Peace after Abortion.*[15] My choice to heal from my abortion was made in God's perfect timing. He knew what I needed, when it was needed, and how to deliver the help gently with compassion. Sydna is a shining example of the Light of Jesus in this world. The following resources were birthed out of her pain and healing to help others dealing with the aftermath of abortion: herchoicetoheal.com, ramahinternational. org, and ramahsvoice.com.

There are times when a traumatic experience can be suppressed for years without us consciously knowing we have been wounded or traumatized. I discovered that our minds and bodies "remember" pain whether we are consciously aware of that pain or not. My post-abortion experience has proven that my life was forever altered on September 12, 1974, when the pregnancy was terminated. It is incomprehensible to me now that I was blinded to the reality of the choice I had made—and to how much it would wound me in the years to come.

God forgives abortion. I am so grateful that God is grace-giving and compassionate. It was imperative for me to humbly and immediately walk through the process of healing and accept forgiveness from God the moment the reality of this sin engulfed me. Forgiving myself was the most difficult part of the process. I can now speak about this experience without being ashamed, through obedience and God's promises. "Be strong and courageous. Do not be afraid or terrified because of them, for the LORD your God goes with you; he will never leave you nor forsake you" (Deuteronomy 31:6).

This book wouldn't be complete if I did not include in the pages the missing piece of my soul. I chose to give my aborted child a name, Jeremiah. The name was chosen after reading about the prophet Jeremiah in the Bible. Jeremiah was part of me and will be a part of my life forever. It is no coincidence that I was given the assignment to write this book. God had to sneak in the inclusion of this chapter. I cannot imagine my horror if I had known ahead of time what God had in store to reveal to me, much less to have me share with others! If I had only allowed others to see the good and polished-looking Brenda, this book would have been only fluff. I wouldn't have seemed credible, I would have felt like a fake, and I would have lost the freedom to write this book without inhibitions. Being real is the way Jesus lived, and being real is the way God longs for us to live our lives.

I still have the gift of today, which gives me the opportunity to make a difference in the lives of others. It is my hope my experience might bring new insights into the mind and heart of a frightened person who is strongly considering abortion. If a decision for abortion is reversed because of the words I write, Jeremiah's life will have made a profound difference in this world. In addition, if my experience as a survivor can help bring hope, compassion, love, or restoration to any wounded, grieving souls,

Jeremiah's life will have made a profound difference in this world. In the case of those who have never accepted God's gift of love and forgiveness, it is my hope that Jeremiah's story might help lead them into a personal and life-preserving relationship with Jesus Christ (the only One who can give true peace, joy, healing, and life evermore). Thus, Jeremiah's life can make a profound difference and impact many in countless ways. "And we know that God causes all things to work together for good to those who love God, to those who are called according to His purpose" (Romans 8:28 NASB).

God is up to something great. He always is. When a woman (and men suffer too) has come through the numbness-and-denial stage of grief following an abortion, she will need support through hugs, not shrugs; compassion, not lashing; love, not shoves; care, not stares. I am unable to tell another person how to be or to control how they feel when they hear about someone else who has chosen abortion. Being on the other side, I have become empathetic and compassionate toward anyone who is struggling with difficult life issues of any kind. The way other people respond or react is between them and God. We can make the choice to love a person unconditionally even when we disagree with their negative behaviors or decisions.

My hope and prayers are that the silent and suffering will find trusted confidantes or support groups who will encourage and lift them up as they choose to heal spiritually, emotionally, physically, and mentally and become whole. Healing begins with a decision, commitment, and honesty on each individual's part in addition to being willing to reach out for help. Placing ourselves in another person's shoes momentarily can give us a broader perspective of this wide world that is filled with hurting people.

Blessings and Peace,
Brenda Eller

Additional Notes to Memo: Not Random

"Those who look to him for help will be radiant with joy; no shadow of shame will darken their faces."

—Psalm 34:5 NLT

It took every ounce of courage I could muster to share "Memo: Not Random" with our adult children and their spouses. As I stumbled through the verbal reading while sobbing and sopping up my tears, I didn't know what to expect from the people closest to me. All I knew was I couldn't hold the secret inside any longer. Through my tear-drenched and blurry eyes, I witnessed the love of God pouring out through my children and their spouses in a way I had never experienced before. Their responses were filled with love, understanding, warmth, acceptance, and much-needed hugs. The strength, comfort, and inspiration I received that night were godsends. Feeling like a fake the rest of my life was not the way I desired to live. If I had gone to the grave with this untold secret, my children would have missed out on knowing their authentic mom.

Kristyn was away at college during that reading, and I let her read "Memo: Not Random" when we were alone together. Many chains were broken on that momentous day. Her knowledge about this traumatic experience in my life cleared the way for an openness between us that wouldn't have been possible otherwise. My courage and authenticity helped resolve many unanswered questions for her. Otherwise, I fear, my overprotective motherly instincts would have pushed us further apart. Kristyn and I would have continued to be clueless about one another's deepest selves if I hadn't sucked it up and shared this part of my life story with her. This was a very important piece in putting our family-life puzzle together for the better.

From the outside, people perceived our family of five as the perfect family who had everything going for us, but nobody can see behind closed doors. Members of our extended family were shut out from the truth by my need to protect and preserve my image. They believed in a version of me that wasn't in alignment with reality.

My sister-in-law, Deenen, opened up to me after reading "Memo: Not Random" several years ago. Recently, I received a text from her that propelled me to keep pushing this book forward in its developmental stages. Her supportive and encouraging words confirm that I'm not alone.

I just think it's awesome that you can open up and be vulnerable. It's sad that we (people) can't open up. Especially with family. This is me speaking, so I know it doesn't apply to everyone. That if we do that, others will be disappointed that our marriages or kids are not perfect. For others will see that we are not the perfect wives, moms that they make us out to be. So we just put on the smiles and hide it all within us. Proud of you! That there are people like you that come out of their comfort zones so we can see that we are not alone in daily struggles.

CEASE AND DESIST

The things that one believes
Both in the mind and heart
Should transfer to the deepest core.
Forgiving self is hard.

When God forgives, our God forgets.
Why choose to beat self up?
The weed called doubt keeps creeping in;
It then will interrupt.

On a mission, Satan lies
And tries to trip our thoughts,
Distorting what God says is true
Into what can seem false.

If one could see what's taking place
And who's behind doubt's mask,
The torture we inflict within
Would cease and end real fast.

Flee from thoughts of self-defeat.
Run fast to reach new heights.
Since God forgave, then so should we;
Release thyself. It's right!

Brenda Eller
7/29/2009

MY CROSS TO SHARE

The losses in life have helped me grow up;
Regrets had been holding me down.
I learned that, in life, letting go of regrets
Would bring smiles to my face and not frowns.

God's words to His child were, "Don't be dismayed.
On yourself, do not choose to beat up.
You will make mistakes; learn from them and move on.
Remember the Cross, Bread, and Cup.

My Son died for you and for everyone else;
He paid for it all on the cross.
Your pain He knew well 'cause He bore it Himself.
Rising up, He conquered each loss.

Go take what you've learned and then give it away;
Never forget all I've given to you.
To bury your loss doesn't mean you'll forget;
It reminds you that I helped you through.

Rise up now and live, living straight from your heart.
Pour My love out to others in deed.
I love you, My child. Do not ever give up,
For the cross that you bore was your need."

Brenda Eller

The Brave

"As with many life endeavors, there are more pieces to the story than surface circumstances reveal."

—Erin Miller

10/29/2015, 4:02 a.m.

In pondering some serious yet perplexing puzzle pieces of my life, I realized how quickly fear had swooped down like a hawk and carried my thoughts away on more than one occasion. When I found myself down in the dumps in the place where a myriad of unknowns and unpredictable outcomes live, it was difficult to crawl out of the mess that natural fears had helped create. True concerns for the health and well-being of others, a compelling need to protect others in the name of love, and an intense desire to protect myself from imagined and potential unknowns came into play. When the curtains were up, the cameras were rolling, and hard things were happening in my life and the lives of those I loved, it was difficult to look past the cast of characters to see God at work behind the scenes. *Putting life puzzles together for better* is easy for God because He knows which piece goes where and the necessity of each piece.

Desperate situations from past years affected my family and me, and some were hit harder by the events than others. A flood of new, unexpected thoughts came rushing in after I thought this book was finished. But the magnifying glass called Truth helped me find my way out of the Doubt House—again. That's the place I had instinctively wandered into because it was familiar territory. *My, oh my! How quickly one can forget!* Being on the grounds of the Doubt House may be perceived as an unhealthy place to be, yet the experience proved to be precious. My faith grew deeper and stronger as a result.

Every door I opened in that house was built out of what I believed were facts, yet emotions and natural human reactions led to spiritual hiccups—big ones, the kind that hurt. Jeremiah 29:11–13 says, "For I know the thoughts and plans that I have for you, says the Lord, thoughts and plans for welfare and peace and not for evil, to give you hope in your final outcome. Then you will call upon Me, and you will come and pray to Me, and I will hear and heed you. Then you will seek Me, inquire for, and require Me [as a vital necessity] and find Me when you search for Me with all your heart" (AMPC).

I wandered around the Doubt House awhile because I didn't realize where I was at the time. Every swinging door I opened revealed things that made sense in the beginning. But as I looked around some more, I discovered that my thinking was not in accordance with God's will. The more I saw, the less I believed in the assumptions and predictions of the Doubt House. Things I had perceived as facts were not in keeping with the most important parts of faith, which are trust and belief in God's provision and His ability to care for every detail of our lives. There was no evidence of complete trust and surrender to God's will when I was on that property. Why had I returned to that life-sapping place again? How could I believe in something I could not know for sure?

When I was growing up, my earthly daddy used to tell me, "Don't think; know." Now, my heavenly Daddy whispered words of comfort and hope to my heart that He knows, He cares, and He is in control of everything. No worries, please.

I prayed, "Dear Lord, please forgive me for falling prey to schemes of the devil. I believe. I believe. In You, I place my trust. In Jesus' name. Amen."

The people that God plants in our paths are there for a reason. Each serves a higher purpose. It is up to us to choose how we will respond to each person's presence in our lives. First, we must identify and adjust, if needed, the attitudes of our hearts toward the people God has sent. When followers act with certainty of God's plans, with strong minds and the attitudes of servants, we can watch God at work without human interference or interruption.

The servant hearts of a God-ordained and God-appointed married couple will now be shared by our eldest daughter, Erin. As she shares impactful and heartwarming mommy moments, tummy times, and heartstrings with us, I ask you to pray deeply for Erin's family since the toughest roller-coaster ride of their lives has only just begun. I am honored to be on the roller-coaster ride with Erin and her dear family.

In the years before Erin and Eric's children arrived, my heart ached for both of them. After their Christmas tree had been decorated year after year, and before each Christmas Day arrived, a small baby doll sat under the tree, leaning against the wrapped presents. I can imagine them carefully positioning the longing in their hearts under the tree in the solitude and quietness of their home.

Before their tree was taken down and the decorations had been stored away for the following year, the baby doll needed to be picked up first. Throughout the seasons, I felt my heart break again and again every time I visited them and looked toward the fireplace. Sitting on the hearth was the baby doll that represented their future child or children. The doll was kept in a prominent place to remind them to pray for their future child, the "hoped-for" birth mom and her pregnancy, and Erin and Eric's future roles as parents. Since then, it has been my joy and immense pleasure to witness the placement of two amazing children into our family, both of them at two weeks of age.

I want to share with you, Erin, that I've told countless people that you and Eric have the biggest hearts I've ever seen. We are so proud of you and the amazing contributions and impacts you make in this world, in our hearts, and in your precious sons' lives. As individuals and a faithful married team, you are brave, sacrificial, selfless, tender, and loving. I look up to you even though you are both shorter than me. You carry loads I would never have been able to carry. God's grace and strength are always enough. Way to go, braves!

Now, Erin would like to share important parts of her family's story with the readers of this book.

Erin's Story

I had no idea the magnitude of my vows to my husband Eric when I spoke them at the altar as a nineteen-year-old bride on November 23, 2002. We were so in love and just wanted to follow the next step the Lord had for us to take. We had our dreams and ideas about what our new life together might look like, but God certainly had a different story to write.

As is the case for most couples, part of our dream together was raising a family. I actually wanted twelve children! Yep! I would still love to have a house full of children. Eric and I talked during our engagement about adopting one day, hoping to have the chance to love both biological and adopted children. Little did we know how our talk of adoption would plant seeds that would grow and bloom into the beautiful family we have today.

The end of February 2008 was tough. A call from my husband came through to my classroom. He was in extreme pain and needed to be rushed to the hospital. That day ended with emergency surgery that solved the mystery of why we still did not have children. The details of that event are personal, but I can say the pain we felt on that day continued through the years. Let's just say that infertility is a loss that cuts deeply.

We did not speak to many people about our infertility news, because it was just too hard and uncomfortable. If that is you, know that you are not alone. Mother's Day at church, baby dedications, and baby showers were the worst. Do not even get me started on all the times people asked us when we were going to have kids! Every question reopened a painful wound.

Even in the hurt and pain, God was there. He used that loss to deepen our burden for children already born and in need of loving, forever families.

Our vision for adoption was to travel overseas to adopt a baby from Ukraine. Working through a local adoption agency seemed like a perfect plan, but we were living then in "married without children" seminary housing. We decided to wait until we moved out to pursue adoption.

We relocated to another state in April 2009 so my husband could become the college and education pastor at a church. One of the college girls attending the college ministry that fall worked as a nanny for a leader of an international orphan-hosting organization. They were looking for host families, and guess which country the children were from. Ukraine! What?! No way!

We ended up hosting two beautiful Ukrainian seven and ten-year-old sisters for a month around Christmases 2009 and 2010. We felt as if they were our girls, and Eric and I pursued adopting them. We had envisioned adopting younger children, but the Lord had opened our hearts to the need for adoptive parents to take in older children. Our paperwork was almost ready to send to Ukraine when we received word that the door had been shut on the Ukrainian side due to unforeseen circumstances. Our paper pregnancy abruptly ended in a difficult miscarriage on March 24, 2011. We were heartbroken at the loss of our girls . . . or what we thought was a loss.

Years later, our Ukrainian "daughters" found us on social media. We learned that they had ended up being raised in the orphanage. They have now graduated from high school and are pursuing college degrees. Throughout the years, we have been able to encourage and support them. They even call me Mom. All those years ago, who would have guessed that we would later help them flee their hometown to seek refuge in a safer city during a brutal war? God sure did! I speak with the oldest girl on a regular basis and get to love both girls through prayer, encouragement, advocacy, and support. Our Ukrainian daughters might not have "Miller" attached to their names through legal adoption, but they are forever part of our family.

During our time of grieving the perceived loss of our Ukrainian girls, my husband and I took time to pray and read Scripture. As we sought the Lord's next steps for our family, I was approached by a church member who wanted to share her adoption story. I learned that her son had been adopted domestically as an infant. I went home and looked at the website of the agency she had used, and there I found her video! As I listened to her adoption story, I really felt this was something God wanted Eric and me to pursue. We talked it over, and before we knew it, we were reaching out to that agency.

Our second paper pregnancy began on October 24, 2011, the day our portfolio was finally submitted for birth mothers to view. That pregnancy was long and hard. It felt like God was pruning us and preparing us for what He already knew would come our way. God's timing is always perfect, but sometimes waiting was hard. However, we had an incredible and godly caseworker who kept us grounded and focused on what really mattered. She encouraged us to enjoy each other in our time of waiting and to keep on living. She urged us not to miss what was right in front of us instead of spending our time wishing for the future. Looking back, I am so thankful for all those years Eric and I got to spend together and grow together without children.

Our caseworker once told us that she often felt like Santa Claus because she knows secrets about adoption plans but has to wait until just the right time to unveil them. That sparked an idea in our heads: "If our caseworker is like Santa, let's put up our Christmas tree early." That's exactly what we did! Our tree went up on October 24 that year. That was the day our portfolio became available to birth mothers, making it the day our caseworker began her role as our Santa.

Eric and I happened to have a baby doll from the time we hosted our Ukrainian girls. We thought it would be fitting to place the baby doll under our early Christmas tree—because a baby would be the perfect Christmas present. The doll also served as a prayer reminder.

Christmas came and went with no real baby. We considered leaving our Christmas tree up until the completion of our adoption waiting process, but the tree came down on New Year's Day. The baby doll moved from under the Christmas tree to its new home on the hearth. It remained there as our prayer reminder until the real baby entered our living room.

The real baby was born on December 10, 2012. We met our son Elijah (Eli) on December 22 and brought him home that same day. How cool is it that after all that time of viewing our caseworker as Santa Claus, she eventually shared with us the amazing Christmas gift of a baby boy! That definitely gave a whole new meaning to celebrating the birth of baby Jesus. It gave me a new understanding of what Mary and Joseph must have felt that first Christmas.

Eli's infancy and toddler years were challenging since he was born with a clubfoot. Weekly casting led to several years of special braces, which got him by until he had surgery when he was seven. In addition, as he grew older, we became aware our son had learning and processing differences. He is now nine years old. Eli is creative, athletic, and compassionate. He cares about others and knows how to make us laugh and smile. He appreciates stopping to smell the flowers and watch the birds, just like his adoptive Grandmom-E!

Eric and I felt led to pursue another adoption in early 2014. By the next January, we learned we had been matched with a baby girl. We even saw a picture of the beautiful little girl and named her. But the birth mother decided to raise her after all, so we were soon back on the waiting list . . . another paper-pregnancy miscarriage.

As it turned out, however, what seemed on paper to be another failed adoption was not a fail at all. God had a perfect plan. Our future second son was growing inside his mommy's tummy while he was growing inside our hearts.

Eric and I had the special gift of meeting our second son's tummy mommy in early April of 2015. We got to hear about her hopes and dreams for her baby, and I could sense her deep love for the son she carried. I remember her asking us what we would want to name him, and we said "Ezekiel." We were overjoyed to learn later that month that she had given birth to her son and named him Ezekiel!

We met baby Ezekiel (Zeke) on April 28, 2015, when he was only twelve days old. It was so amazing to make the trip home that day as a family of four.

Zeke was the calmest and chillest baby I had ever met (or at least that is what I thought). His very energetic and loud two-year-old brother did not even faze him. Without voicing our worries to each other, Eric and I both started wondering if Zeke could hear or see. He was having trouble keeping his food down, and we noticed unusual movements, which concerned us. By the time he was around four months old, our pediatrician referred Zeke for testing since he still was not following objects with his eyes and his head was not growing.

The end of August 2015 rocked our world. My mom came over to watch Eli while Eric and I took Zeke to the eye doctor. It was that visit that set everything in motion. I will never forget the image of the doctor sitting at the desk just staring at his papers for a while. I knew something was not right. Finally, the doctor turned to us and told us our son could not see.

So many emotions welled up in us; we were blindsided by the news. I looked up Zeke's eye condition online and learned that children with that diagnosis often have a long list of other issues. I got on the phone and stayed on it until specialist appointments were lined up.

God opened the door for Zeke to see a neurologist the following week, just one month before his adoption finalization date! See, even from the beginning,

God was in this! Had we found out about Zeke's condition after the court had finalized our adoption, we would not have been able to secure appropriate resources for his long-term care. It is also super rare to get into a neurologist's office that quickly. God orchestrated that appointment in His perfect timing! The neurologist examined Zeke and ordered an EEG for the next week. During the EEG, the tech stopped the test halfway through the process and sent us upstairs to meet with the neurologist again. We knew something was not right.

I remember looking around the waiting room at all the patients and wondering what my son might come to have in common with them as the years went on. I saw behaviors that were different from the norm, and I saw a child in a wheelchair. This was not the kind of waiting room I was accustomed to visiting. What was going on?

When our turn came to see the doctor, he shared with us that Zeke had infantile spasms, a rare seizure disorder in infants that sends the brain into complete and constant chaos. He sent us directly to the hospital.

That hospital stay turned out to be the first of many. That hospital stay was the start of a very hard road.

Zeke was put on a seizure medication that had devastating side effects. Infantile spasms are difficult to treat and require aggressive measures because of the terrible long-term damage they can cause. That medication made our sweet and happy Zeke disappear. He became a miserable vegetable for a long time.

One appointment after another led to the unveiling of a longer list of issues. Our adoption agency knew that we had not signed up for a child with special needs. The "perfectly healthy child" they had placed in our home was not healthy after all. Representatives from our agency came to our home to discuss the situation. They gave us an out. They said we did not have to do this and that they could find another family for Zeke.

Eric and I worked through this and prayed and sought counsel. We knew the adoption would require enormous sacrifices and result in a very different kind of life than the one we were used to. However, Zeke was our son. I believe God kept multiple doctors from seeing Zeke's differences at first because it allowed us to fall madly in love with him before learning about his unique needs. By that point, he had our hearts; we were willing to do whatever was necessary to care for our sweet Zeke.

In that time of decision, God reminded me that He had adopted *me* into His family with all my different needs. Who was I to say "no" to adopting Zeke because he had needs as well?

We laid our strong "*Yes!*" on the table and continued our pursuit of Zeke's adoption.

We had a rocky start to 2016. Zeke grew sick. A hospital stay in January revealed that Zeke had been silently aspirating, meaning some of his food was going into his lungs instead of into his stomach. Zeke went home with a feeding tube, never to eat by mouth again.

That same month, Eric and I learned that the finalization of Zeke's adoption would take an additional year to complete due to his newly diagnosed needs. Most everything had to be put on hold that year until the adoption was official.

That entire February was spent in the pediatric intensive care unit (PICU). Zeke was so sick we honestly thought it was goodbye. During that stay, a PICU doctor sat down with Eric and me in a conference room. He knew we were pursuing Zeke's adoption and wanted us to be well informed about what was going on with him. The doctor drew a picture of Zeke's brain and explained what had likely happened. He also gave us the tough news that kids like Zeke normally are unable to do anything and usually do not live past the age of three.

That was tough to hear, but we did not waver from our decision. Zeke was worth fighting for, and he deserved to be loved.

We continued our PICU stay while Zeke recovered from his illness. That stay illuminated Zeke's fragility and the need for additional long-term support. That was when he became officially classified as a medically fragile child. Zeke left the hospital with a suction machine, a physical therapy machine to be used on his chest, a permanent feeding tube, and arrangements for in-home nursing care.

As the year continued, we learned of new challenges Zeke faced, including hearing loss. God connected us with amazing therapists to teach and train us how to care for a medically fragile deaf and blind child.

Zeke's adoption was officially finalized in January of 2017. We were so excited to have Zeke as an official Miller forever!

We were eventually given a main diagnosis for Zeke; he has an extremely rare CASK gene variant. Zeke has microcephaly (small head), a small cerebellum, a movement disorder, a history of seizures, feeding tube dependency, a tendency to aspirate, obstructive sleep apnea, lung disease, asthma, neurogenic bladder requiring catheterization, reflux, low muscle tone, wheelchair dependency, severe developmental delays, several eye conditions that have left him legally blind, and hearing loss. He is nonverbal as well, and the list continues to grow. Zeke requires total care.

It has been quite a journey. Zeke is now seven and amazes us all the time with his progress! Despite his adversities and what was predicted in the past, Zeke is thriving! He expresses emotions such as laughing when happy and crying when upset. He uses a Pragmatic Organization Dynamic Display (PODD) system and switch device to communicate his wants and needs. For example, he has learned the PODD pathways to request a car ride, an outdoor walk, and a hug. He is growing like a weed . . . the good kind of weed as Grandmom-E would say! His hearing has significantly improved. He is becoming more alert and is more aware of his surroundings. He has definitely far surpassed the PICU doctor's prediction!

Looking back, I can see how God was preparing my garden so I could help my sons bloom in gardens of their own.

As a classroom teacher, I was always drawn to my struggling students. I sat in countless Individualized Education Plan (IEP) meetings and worked closely with my students to help meet their needs. My love for those with special needs began in church. I remember sitting a few rows back from the Promise Class every Sunday morning. I always felt love for them and had an interest in their needs. I volunteered in that class as a youth and later almost majored in special education. Even as a student, I was drawn to my classmates who needed extra help or seemed to be alone. I have always found satisfaction in standing up for others and being an advocate. Little did I know that the Lord was growing seeds in my heart to nurture my own children. Now I am the parent in the IEP meetings, the mom of the child in the special classes, and the constant advocate.

God did not just prepare my garden; He made my garden thrive. He did not just prepare me to help my boys bloom, but He has used adoption to help me bloom.

Adoption has enabled me to see the truth of God's gospel on constant display right in front of me. I cannot help but think of the Lord when I see my boys. When opportunities arise for me to share with Eli that my husband and I *chose* him to be in our family, I cannot help but draw closer to the Lord—who chose *me* and loves me unconditionally.

Parenting a medically fragile child has shifted my entire perspective on life. I value life more, and I cherish the gift of every moment as I see clearly every day just how fragile and fleeting life can be. I think more about what is really important instead of sweating the small stuff. I have a greater sense of gratitude. I have a deeper appreciation for the truth that every life matters. God has a purpose for everyone, no matter what their differences might be. My dependence on the Lord has definitely increased. I cannot do what I do as a mom without the Lord's help. The name Ezekiel actually means "God strengthens." It is not just Zeke who needs God's strength—it is also me!

God continues growing my garden through the relationship side of adoption. I would love to one day develop a relationship with Eli's tummy mommy, and I am glad I have been able to cultivate a connection with Zeke's tummy mommy. She found me on social media and started a conversation. I admit, I was scared and closed off at first to the notion of communicating, but being able to communicate with each other has blossomed into a garden of blessings. We talk occasionally through private messages, and I even share stories and pictures with her through a private social media platform. Zeke's amazing tummy mommy has been a source of encouragement! She sees that God placed Zeke into our family for a reason, and I totally agree. This has been a story only God could write!

My mom calls me brave for adopting, but I call my sons' tummy mommies the brave ones. Read on to find out why.

5/9/2015

Edited post from an adoption blog I used to manage . . .

Their Names Mean Brave

Behind every cover of a book is a story. Behind every play is a director. Behind every door is a gateway. Behind every adoption is a heart—the heart of a birth mom, the heart of the adoptive child, the heart of the adoptive parent, the heart of the adoptive family's caseworker, the heart of the birth mother's caseworker. So much goes on behind the scenes of an adoption. My sons did not just land on my front doorstep with the help of a stork or postal worker. Adoption involves prayer, patience, and sacrifice. Adoptive families make sacrifices to adopt, but birth mothers are the ones who truly exemplify sacrifice.

I signed my name as a witness when a birth mother completed her adoption paperwork in November. I saw her hold her son for the last time as she sat on her hospital bed and signed her adoption-plan papers. Ten days after that, her parental rights were officially surrendered, allowing her son to enter into the care of a family she lovingly chose for him. As one of the four people to sign those papers and watch as the birth mother's pen formed a life-changing signature, I felt my love for birth moms grow.

My signature was also on the greeting card we gave Zeke's birth mother along with a bouquet of flowers when we met with her in early April. I saw her expressions as she spoke with us. I heard her heart as she asked important questions regarding her son's future. I will never forget the words she softly spoke about her hopes and dreams for her son. I maintained my composure, but inside I was crying the tears she was fighting back. Zeke's Birth Mom, your son will always hear from us about how much you love him! That meeting showed another layer of pain and loss that birth mothers face. It also showed another layer of love that birth mothers give.

My name was also signed onto the adoption papers that allowed us to bring Eli and Zeke into our family. My name there signified that I was now the forever mom of these two amazing boys. That completed signature line indicated that motherly responsibilities were now upon me. I gladly welcomed them—the commitments I was making and the sons who were now mine. I grieved along with the birth mothers who were mourning their losses. Again, my love and admiration for birth mothers grew.

Theirs were the signatures that gave me two amazing gifts called Elijah and Ezekiel. Their names I remember. Their names I admire. Their names mean "brave."

Sparkles

"Many years ago, my mother taught me a godly principle: 'To share is one of the greatest joys possible.'"

—Barbara Cooke

Only God knows how and when each of our life stories will end. Until my time comes, I will give the precious gift called life everything I have and squeeze the juice and joy out of every moment. Because of all that God has done for me, I will serve as He directs me, no matter how or when, without questioning His expertise on the subject that really matters—life.

"Make us to choose the harder right instead of the easier wrong
and never to be content with a half truth when the whole
can be won."[16]

—Col. Clayton E. Wheat, The "Cadet Prayer"

The future is full of opportunity, not gloom and doom, dread or fret. Difficult situations, people, and events will grow us up in ways that will reveal underlying potential we otherwise would have never been able to experience or share.

God led me to a quiet and sacred place on a mountain to be alone in His presence without distractions or interference from the outside world. Along with embarking on my healing journey, I was preparing the cabin for future guests and occupants. Multiple visits were a requirement since it was impossible to bring the cabin to my "Fix-It Shoppe" at home. My physical presence was needed at the location where the cabin was planted and growing. I grew to appreciate the cabin. It was a place that needed help, and the time at the cabin helped me deal with my feelings about the abortion.

My thoughts wandered back to 2010, before the land was purchased. A seed had been planted in Gary's heart and mind to build a cabin. I took the stance of "going along to get along." Being a supportive wife was the way I chose to respond to that unexpected situation. I would have been content with one home, the one in which we lived, but "we" set out on a venture with twists neither of us could have foreseen at the time. In the process, God caused greater good to grow out of the garden of the soul. He was taking each piece and putting them together in the way He knew was best.

On February 11, 2011—three months before construction on the cabin began—I started training to be a volunteer at our local pregnancy resource center. As The Blest Nest's structure expanded and was taking form, Gary needed my help since he was still working full-time. I struggled to keep up with the growing demands at the cabin. Realizing I wasn't able to donate my time in two places, I brought my service at the resource center to an end when my labors at The Blest Nest increased.

At the time, I didn't understand why "we" suddenly had to build a cabin, but now it makes perfect sense. God was the biggest and most important part of "we." He knows our needs and blessed me with the perfect place to work on personal healing. Wounds from my past were creatively being tended to, one layer and one story at a time.

On July 15, 2011, Gary was on a hiking trip, and I decided to enter "Brenda World" again. It was invigorating to walk through the cabin, then under construction, without another person being on the property. The serene atmosphere blessed my soul with peace, but the stay, unfortunately, had a not-so-peaceful end. It was getting late, and the time to head back to the real world had arrived. I had used various sizes of scrap wood to create a tall stepping stool since I was too short to get on and off the back porch without assistance. When I stepped down off the deck, the stepping stool fell apart during my descent. I fell backward and, in trying to break my fall, broke my wrist. Thankfully, it was my left wrist, so I could still drive myself home while carefully shifting gears.

Taking photos of the cabin's progress with my right hand was easy, but trying to spread peanut butter on a cracker was painful. Opening a can of paint and picking up a brush was a ridiculous idea to consider in my condition. Still, surprisingly, I found unexpected benefits. Even though I felt helpless in physical ways, I was given blessings I would have otherwise missed. Being able to keep my mouth shut when frustrations would have normally led me to step in helped me take my place on the sidelines at the cabin and not interfere with things I could not change (not then, anyway).

I chose to focus on the interior's design. Learning how to furnish and decorate a log cabin proved to be time well spent. Researching ideas on the internet was challenging and time-consuming yet delightful. It kept me busy while my broken wrist healed.

From the cabin's early construction stages, I chose to enjoy the process, maintain a generous and cheerful attitude, and trust God with the results. I gave purposeful attention to the details because it was not just a cabin. (I knew that fact deep down inside. There was a *knowing*.) The cabin was birthed to be a sacred, set-apart place where God could speak life, love, and peace into individual hearts. I was determined to value and treat it with the respect it deserved. Doing all that is necessary to bring something up to a standard of excellence is important to me.

On July 17, 2012, before the doors were officially opened to receive guests, a quiet visitor appeared on the property wearing a coat of brown. Even though we had received a certificate of occupancy from the county, I knew the cabin was *not* ready for The Blest Nest guests. I had already spent months getting the cabin ready for people, and there was still more work to be done. But when I first laid eyes on my new feathery friend, it didn't matter that the cabin wasn't ready for people, because Sparkles was a bird! Nothing else mattered at that moment, not even time. I stood still, then I watched Sparkles silently teach. Even without the help of a guest book, I witnessed the message the little bird brought to my heart and learned from the understanding I received.

The bird's name was inspired by one of my favorite trees on the property —a beautiful sparkleberry tree that always made me smile. As with the tree, there was something special about the bird. Her behavior instantly caught my attention. For the entire day, I thought Sparkles was injured because I didn't see her fly. Instead, Sparkles stayed close to the cabin's foundation and pecked at the ground, finding nourishment from bugs under the soil's surface.

Later that night, I slowly walked around the yard enjoying the beauty of the moonlight illuminating the chestnut oak and sparkleberry trees. I discovered an unusual clump of something next to the cabin's foundation wall that had not been there the night before. After closer inspection, I discovered it was Sparkles! Peacefully sleeping under the light of the moon, the sweet bird had chosen to nestle under the stars in the exact spot where I had repaired the first construction oversight I discovered. Even though the repair had to be made on the exterior foundation wall by digging down several feet, Sparkles knew where and how to apply some needed balm to my healing heart.

I recall a drawing I made of the cabin that had tears falling from the two dormers and trickling down from the windows. The cabin and I connected at the *soul* level. We both needed to be healed from something.

The next day, Sparkles hopped round and round the foundation wall as she had the day before. Instead of staying close to the cabin, the bird ventured out into the yard, pecking at the ground with greater interest and purpose. I remember smiling as I witnessed Sparkles enjoying a *bath* in a puddle of rainwater that had collected between wrinkles of black construction plastic in the yard. It made me happy that the discarded plastic from the crawl space was being used in such a delightful way. I followed my happy friend around the yard and took photos for identification purposes and to keep memories of the day alive. I then began to notice little white things scattered on the ground and around the site of the future driveway but dismissed them as being unimportant.

That night, Sparkles slept under the stars on her personal feather pillow—in the same place she had slept the night before. How fitting for a real bird to be the first overnight guest at The Blest Nest! Our God is so creative. He knew exactly when, where, why, and how the bird and I needed to meet.

I stayed indoors the next morning since the driveway was being poured. After the workers were through and about to leave for the day, I went outside to talk with Ronnie Hall, our driveway-paving expert. During our conversation, he asked, "Did you happen to see a little bird around here the past few days? It looked hurt, so we gave it breadcrumbs from our breakfast yesterday. I thought it was injured and couldn't fly. But then we saw it again today. All of a sudden, it just flew off into those woods. We haven't seen it since."

Awesome! Each of us had a personalized experience with Sparkles. We were all excited to know Sparkles was well enough to fly. God knew all about His feathery creation and provided for Sparkles' daily needs (love, protection, clothing, food, shelter, and rest). Sparkles also is the nickname I've adopted for myself, because the feathered friend I met at the cabin inspired me to take a break from busyness and choose to enjoy the simplest of things. Sparkles helped me pause, be still, process all that I've experienced, and evaluate what is really important in this life.

The twinkling of light manifested through a tiny friend for several days in the quietness and stillness of a mountain setting was enlightening. Nature reveals its secrets to those who observe with attentiveness and can appreciate truths that hold a deeper purpose. Sweet memories of Sparkles continue to enliven me today.

AUGUST 2012

Gary had recently turned the rental and management of the cabin over to me. Our dog, Beau, and I enjoyed being the first "couple" to savor the serenity of The Blest Nest overnight. Somebody had to take care of our furry family member, and I was elected by default. As crazy as it may sound, it was exciting to load the car down with tools and supplies to work on finishing the trim, doors, walls, windows, and whatever else might need attention. After I packed other essentials, Beau and I headed to the cabin for work, companionship, and peace.

Kristyn and I had chosen the fluffy white, curly-haired, precious bichon frise pup when he was six weeks old. She needed a buddy to fill the void after her sister went away to college. Beau was a welcomed emotional support dog for both of us. We related to him in different ways, and his presence gave us something in common to help us connect.

I will always be grateful for the special memories I had with Beau at the cabin. In addition to hearing raindrops dance atop the cabin's metal roof and peacocks calling to one another in the not-too-distant valley, I heard familiar sounds coming from my furry companion. He snored, slurped, chomped, crunched, licked, and scratched.

Beau knew he was deeply loved. My granddog and I had been friends since March of 2001. When our family needed his energetic and joy-promoting presence to lighten our dark moods, Beau was there.

Beau and I became senior citizens together. Now, he needed geriatric care and attention from one who knew him best. I was the one who needed to provide stability and be his friend until the end. Beau had been the buddy who heard my deepest sobs, felt my hottest tears, and rushed to my side to hug me the best way he could, allowing me to hold him when nobody else was around to fill that need. Animals seem to know when we need them the most. They are forgiving by nature and will never, ever spill a secret to anyone. Beau didn't try to fix anything; he couldn't. He just listened, and I knew he heard my heart. When Beau looked at me during those vulnerable times, the windows to his soul comforted me. My heart heard him say, "It's going to be okay." And I knew eventually it would.

Beau passed from this life on August 20, 2012. The sparkles he left behind will remain in our hearts forever. Sometimes all you or I need is a spark to jump-start our hearts and set them in the direction of our finest destiny.

My time alone with God at the cabin was precious. I recognized the source of my help and experienced God's strength as He took the jagged and gut-wrenching parts of my life to create a beautiful home to be used in His way, not ours. The cabin was a refuge for me as I worked through the grieving process related to my abortion.

Forgiveness and reconciliation with difficult people from my past were incorporated into works of art at the cabin. Prayers were written on the back sides of woodwork. Unconditional love was expressed in the form of smiley faces drawn with leftover Perma-Chink Energy Seal® Textured Caulk I kept on hand for repairs. Hammering in protruding nails and sanding woodwork symbolized the removal of anything that could harm another person. No *sharps* were allowed to remain at The Blest Nest. I eradicated anything that was negative in any way, which helped to make the cabin fit for queens, kings, and their offspring. Hopefully, you get the idea behind why I did the things

I did and why it took so long. Healing takes time, yet I was given the blessed gift of doing just that so Gary and I could, as a couple, pay forward all that God has done for us.

Many memories were made at the cabin, and I've chosen to hold on to those that still bring me joy. Essential endings are a part of life, and so are refreshing new beginnings. Breaking free from all that binds is necessary to experience life the way God intended.

12/26/2021

When I view the experience of the cabin as a whole, I see a beautiful work of art birthed out of pain. The labor of love was worth going through everything "we" went through in order to pass the property on to the next homeowner baggage-free. The Blest Nest represents the garden of the soul. The following is Gary's initial comment in reference to that representation: "The battle occurred on the hill. We drove away and never looked back." After sleeping on his words last night, I began waking up through the night like popcorn in a kettle, needing to write down the messages I received with each "pop." (The proverbial bowl of revealed messages required me to closely examine the messages and discern which subjects that matter could be publicly shared. Whittling unnecessary details from this chapter was difficult yet freeing. This chapter needed to go through several "surgeries" to remove parts that could taint the whole. During each surgery, I used scissors to cut out words that needed to be shredded. Taping the remaining pieces together helped me be a peacemaker instead of stirring up hurtful things from the past.)

Spiritual warfare had taken place on the hill. Through it all, God was fighting our battles and defeating the enemy, who had relentlessly been challenging Gary and me. I hold on tightly to this promise in Isaiah 54:17: "No weapon formed against you shall prosper" (NKJV). Each mess contained a message, each test became a part of our testimony, which can help others; and each trial ended with us being able to give God the glory for bringing us through the storms and helping us become better people.

Gary's words changed overnight. He now describes our experience at the cabin in this way: "Victory was completed at the battle on the hill." We didn't begin the cabin venture with any suspicion that a battle would later show up on our doorstep. Yet, there we were and there it was. It was through divine intervention that Gary was able to bring the seven-year-and-eight-month season to a close. Deuteronomy 20:4 brings promise, hope, and reassurance: "For the Lord your God is going with you! He will fight for you against your enemies, and he will give you victory!" (NLT).

Unexpected situations occur. Each has a beginning and will ultimately come to an end. It's how we respond to those situations that can turn victims into victors. Holding on to the promises of God instead of focusing on all that's going wrong around us will keep us on track every time. A narrow focus on specific details doesn't allow us time to think about the most important facts that can help us see the broadest view.

It was helpful for me to look back over the cabin experiences with the healthiest perspective possible. The cabin's existence was an important part of my life. My soul was being prepared to receive God's healing. When I flew away from The Blest Nest after my work there had been accomplished, I didn't know where God would lead me or what He was calling me to do. But I do know that I am healed through Christ and that I can *fly off into those woods* with God's provision, protection, guidance, and love. I will keep on flying and gliding for a lifetime, no matter what comes my way in the future.

How do I know that? A little birdie told me, "Divinely sparkle! Peace will glow!"

"Life is unpredictable and often unfair. We must travel that winding road of loss and disappointment to discover inner strength, peace, and even joy."[17]

—Jill Smith Entrekin

Our Lady Cave

We can be scammed into believing anything when we leave the research up to others who may not know the truth or have our best interests in mind or heart. Through the years, I've encountered individuals I mistakenly believed could be trusted to give solid and helpful advice. They may have been misinformed, failed to listen attentively, or didn't genuinely care. Tough experiences have taught me not to believe everything I hear and to keep on searching until I find what feels right, sounds right, and has a proven rate of success.

SPRING 2011

Gears were turning in my mind as I stood gazing at the exposed crawl space, which had no roof at the time. A casual observer would have seen concrete foundation walls and three support piers on the cabin's building site. I saw them too, but my mind dug deeper. I'm not a casual observer regarding most things. Lumps, rocks, and roots were visible in the dry, compacted soil. Based on past experiences working with undisturbed soil, I knew that additional rocks, roots, and sticks could explain the lumpy terrain. I was also concerned because a nearby tree had to be removed before the footings could be poured. A log cabin could make many termites happy!

I longed to prepare the area properly to create valuable, usable space. Taking advantage of the opportunity to enter the crawl space while one could stand up straight, not hit their head, and not have to crawl wasn't on anyone's radar screen except mine. My idea of clearing the area of unwanted debris would certainly be shot down as soon as the words exited my mouth, so I kept quiet. In my mind, I knew this job had my name written all over it, so I waited for the right time to do the work under the cabin, when nobody would be on the property to cause static or intervene without invitation.

The reason for doing the clearing had to be good enough that no one could dispute my purpose. We don't always welcome the countless lessons that cultivate patience, yet they are needed. In considering this situation from a higher perspective, I recalled the words of the Down-to-Earth Wise Owl who helped me realize I needed to wait until the time was right: "Whoooever takes the higher road brings to the table lighter loads." Two inaudible words, *not now,* gave me hope and helped me keep my dream alive.

2012–2013

A crawl space is normally not the place a lady would choose to make into her designated special space, yet this lady did. I was forced to go where some people would never think about entering unless they had to. I dared myself to go into the crawl space because it had conjured up fear and creepy feelings within. Living things can grow, slither, crawl, and hop in environments that give them the opportunity to hide and thrive unnoticed and undetected.

The crawl space in our newly constructed vacation/rental cabin needed help. Someone had to "go there" to find out what was not right in the place down under. All contractors and inspectors had considered their jobs at The Blest Nest to be complete in March of 2012, yet what was deemed to be acceptable wasn't—in multiple ways.

Some oversights were immediately addressed, yet other areas of concern weren't discovered until a significant amount of time had elapsed. For instance, I was grateful I was in the cabin when torrential rains pounded against the walls. After discovering water on the bathroom floor, I found where it was coming from. Water was running down the wall from both sides of the window. Thankfully, the water had not reached the hickory floors outside the bathroom. For forty minutes, I held two bath towels against the wall to keep the rainwater contained. Then I called a professional window installer to assess the problem. His findings were that none of the lower windows had been sealed with exterior flashing tape. It wasn't there! After that problem was corrected and repairs had been made, I chose not to become bitter. Instead, I proceeded to help make things at the cabin better instead of turning a blind eye toward any problem presented. I dove in on all fours (at times, literally) and tackled each concern with the mindset and attitude of a caring contractor, picky inspector, loving laborer, and willing grunt lady.

If I was unable to tackle a task personally, we paid true professionals who could. Some jobs required much more than I could deliver or more than I was willing to do. The internet was a valuable resource I utilized often to find the most effective ways to do what needed to be done. In that broad world and among local friends in the building community, I found professionals who were willing to listen to my valid concerns and educate me. This approach left me with new understanding from the minds of masters, hands-on experience, opportunities to add new tools to my toy (I mean "tool") box, and skills to use in future endeavors.

My Lady Cave has a story to tell,
Holding dirt, rocks, and roots in three plastic blue pails.
Its beginning was subtle; science crept up on me.
I was chosen to battle high humidity.

Hickory floors were first to let out their shouts
Like firecrackers drowning out quiet, sweet sounds.
To let crawl space dirt breathe a sigh of relief,
Black plastic was removed, which exposed future grief.

The mud underneath a big PVC pipe
Spoke up and said water had been coming inside.
Some sill plates were moist, and they had to be caulked.
I tried hard to stay calm so I wouldn't balk.

While the dirt was still drying, I noticed some growth.
Fungal spores had been living on then-current hosts.

When mushrooms were visible, I called pros for help.
A plan of attack would soon be unveiled.

I followed advice from pros that I chose
And removed all the dirt that had been exposed.
It served a good purpose outside in low spots.
Donning hazmat attire made good sense on this lot.

My dream of creating good usable space
Could not have been planned with more love and sweet grace.
Nobody could protest; work had to be done.
I chose to enjoy it and have loads of fun.

Like a miner who digs in a quest to find gold,
I dug and I dug to find treasures untold.
Discoveries were made as I dug into mounds.
Tree parts were unearthed; living termites were found.

Untouched cement blobs hugged a foundation wall;
I questioned protection from termites in "crawl."
After phone calls were made, a pro tested the dirt.
The crawl space failed miserably; I chose not to curse.

Termiticide waited till I finished my task.
At least truth was found, then protection could last.
After treatment, remediators began their fine work
To clean, treat, and seal, giving "crawl" a rebirth.

The dirt, rocks, and roots shared great truths that were learned.
Every square inch of "crawl" had been thoroughly searched.
I chose to sow love and walked second miles;
This Lady Cave's heartbeat will be felt a long while.

Two other fitting names for The Blest Nest could be the Blest Mess and the Blest Test, depending on the situation. Attacking the crawl space meant I had to go all in. There was no middle ground. This work wasn't possible standing outside the crawl space door and doing nothing about the true need inside.

Surface mold was visible on the exposed two-by-ten floor joists overhead. High humidity levels had to be addressed with proven ways to remedy the unhealthy situation. Before the black plastic was removed, I was unnerved by the idea of crawling over it, not knowing what was underneath. But I gathered courage and chose to be brave.

Even though my labors of love were motivated by the interests and needs of others, I received countless blessings along my journey toward making the cabin a place of wholeness and peace. My soul was given nourishment only souls are capable of receiving. Accepting and welcoming the monumental task of chiseling out the crawl space in preparation for encapsulation was easy. Sealing the area properly was best left up to professionals. Turning the crawl space into a dry space where mold could not grow was of utmost importance for the health and longevity of the building as a whole. Improving indoor air quality was imperative in order to provide current and future occupants a safe and healthy environment.

I had been being prepared for this feat years before The Blest Nest property was purchased. Instead of the relief carving being performed outdoors, this time the familiar tools were used indoors. The crawl-space vents became tiny windows for airflow. A roof overhead kept dirt and tools dry. A little red wagon was a safe place for my cell phone. An aromatic candle created much-needed ambiance, and solitude blessed my soul with peace.

When I was interviewing professionals about cleaning, treating, protecting, and sealing the area properly, Terry Howell observed he could *feel* the positive energy radiating from My Lady Cave. He said, "Crawl spaces are wonderful places to contemplate the ways of man." Doing all I was doing and hiring trained professionals would enable the crawl space to provide good vibes for the living quarters above.

Blessings in disguise became clear when several men from a different mold remediation company were sitting on the crawl-space floor with me. I noticed one of the men had been looking up, left to right, scanning the horizontal structural beam. Then he looked at me and asked, "Did you know there are no joist hangers on this side of the support beam?"

I replied, "No, I didn't. Thank you!" I was grateful he noticed and cared enough to share. Like I noted before, when areas of concern became known, they were addressed and corrected. Argh!

We can't keep mold spores out of our homes, but we can take measures to avoid giving them opportunities to grow. To stop fungal spores from growing and thriving, one must first solve the moisture problem that allowed the mold to grow in the first place. Mycology is a worthwhile subject to investigate. Our former and current homes are blest recipients of the knowledge I gained after crawling through The Blest Nest's cave entrance.

Tracey Moore, a poet, author, and speaker, pours important truths into our souls with these words: "The thought of living life in this world without God is a scary prospect. Therefore, if we want to hold on to our sanity and regain equilibrium when we have been blindsided, the only answer is this: Trust God. It's the only way out."[18] As it turned out, the misfortunes in the crawl space eventually led to good. Trusting God to take care of things His way, in His time, breathes life into challenges and supports joy in trials.

My Lady Cave was a place to tenderly care for my soul in solitude. It was a place to corral my thoughts, sort them out, and weed out those that needed to be shaken loose and removed. It helped me hold on to life-giving thoughts, which are beneficial and practical in day-to-day living. I agree with Terry Howell that "crawl spaces are wonderful places to contemplate the ways of man."

The name Our Lady Cave was birthed through divine intervention. During the season of preparing My Lady Cave for its best life, additional care was being given to the master suite above. I was in the process of creating a special place for our lady guests (and me) to put on our makeup. Searching for the perfect-size multipurpose shelf was like going on an Easter egg hunt. The shelf was needed to serve as a nightstand and hold candles, coffee, and complementary decor items. Then there it was. Propped up in a corner at a local antique store was the golden egg! After I had secured the antique tigerwood shelf to the bedroom wall, the floating shelf looked incomplete and needed additional support from corbels. I wanted the corbels to represent angel wings since the shelf was part of an "Angels Gather Here" theme I had planned.

A particular store came to mind, and I knew it would be the perfect place to find fitting angel wings. I met Jenni in that store, where I would find more than I could have imagined! Our stories merged at that moment in time and became a beautiful example of God's love and provision. A friendship between us blossomed and grew. God grows the most beautiful friendships and orchestrates the most inspiring symphonies!

Jenni was as eager to please as I was eager to find. As two ladies on an important mission, we became forced to use our "thinking caps." Searching the store, we didn't find anything that resembled angel wings. Then Jenni began to think outside the box and came up with something that might work. The potential angel wings were at her house. She said, "I get off work at five. Could you meet me at the corner gas station, and I'll bring what I have from home and let you decide?"

Shortly after that, she met me with some curtain-rod corbels, and I had my wings. Later, I created a larger backing for the corbels, and the finished angel wings were stunning. Jenni and I thought our mission was accomplished, but God had bigger plans in store for us.

During our search for angel wings, I learned that Jenni and her fiancé, Mike, couldn't find a suitable and budget-friendly venue for their wedding. Since Gary had put me in charge of managing the cabin, I felt comfortable asking Jenni, "What do you think about you and Mike getting married at the cabin? You can also stay there for your honeymoon." I wish you could have seen the relief and excitement on her face!

Jenni invited me to the wedding, and it made me smile to see the cabin's furnishings and decor being used so creatively. I felt honored to be the desig-nated photographer. I was the only person in the cabin with Jenni and her daughters when Jenni's brother started playing the guitar and her sister started singing. As Jenni and her daughters walked toward the screened-in porch, where the ceremony would take place, I instantly recognized the angelic song "When You Say Nothing at All".[19]

Months earlier, our granddaughter Emily had chosen that song for an imaginary wedding at the cabin. That wedding was planned the morning of the "event" itself. On the way to the cabin, we bought a boy doll and a tiny tux. Emily named the future groom Mason. I had recently purchased a CD titled

Selections from the Heart from a dear friend, LaVada Vaillancourt-McCosh. Emily and I were listening to LaVada's CD in the car that "eventful" day. Her song of choice to be played at the wedding was "When You Say Nothing at All." We listened to LaVada sing the song over and over and over until we arrived at the cabin. It was fun watching Emily dream of the wedding-to-be and hearing her sing along with LaVada.

After we arrived at the cabin, Emily looked through the toy box and found "the preacher." Our grandson Noah collected toy figurines, and one of them quickly took on a new identity in Emily's imagination! With the CD player ready, the fashion-doll bride in her place, a photographer on standby (me), and the future bride and groom ready to silently say, "I do," in front of the voiceless preacher, the music began to play. The lyrics to the song were fitting for this event.

I became caught up in Emily's imagination. Watching the tender and graceful expressions of Emily's creativity was like witnessing a real-life wedding. To capture the best photos possible, I had been crawling around on the floor following Emily, who made the dolls walk, talk, and dance together as newlyweds. The top of a six-by-six bedpost became the perfect-size dance floor.

Emily's fairy-tale wedding came true at the cabin a few months later with a real bride and groom saying "I do." When I heard the guitarist playing "When You Say Nothing at All" at Jenni and Mike's wedding, I was speechless and in awe! It was a miraculous confirmation that this real wedding was meant to be and was blessed by God.

I intentionally left the door to Our Lady Cave unlocked so that Jenni and Mike could have the entire property all to themselves. Jenni knew that Gary and I had marital struggles. She offered to write something for me and said she would hide it in a special place for me to find after their stay. Jenni chose to sit alone and write at the desk in Our Lady Cave. The following heartfelt words of advice came from one who chose to pay forward what she had learned from life experiences.

Happiness is a state of mind, yet it is crucial to our everyday lives. What makes one happy? This is a question everyone seeks the answer to, yet very rarely is the answer found. Happiness comes from within and it often comes from things unseen. It is the laughter of a young child, it is the innocence of children, it is the love felt between two people, and it can change your life forever.

The question still arises . . . How do you stay happy in a marriage? The answer is simple: Stay young and continue to grow as one with your spouse. Discover his likes and dislikes, his strengths and weaknesses and focus on him. Make one another laugh and have fun. Act like children once in a while; this will keep your spirits young. Live for each moment and make sacrifices for one another. You only live once, so make it count. Become best friends with your spouse.

Before the twinkle of interest in Gary's eye turned into real plans to build the cabin, God was there. He knew Jenni and I would meet, and He orchestrated events and created needs to make it happen. Jenni was planted in my life for multiple reasons and seasons. Our Lady Cave is proof that great things come about when we're willing to roll up our sleeves, get down on our knees, and pray our way through obstacles that seem to have no end. God played a major part in Our Lady Cave. Jenni was there in spirit long before it began. I'm thankful I kept searching until I found what felt right, sounded right, and had a proven rate of success for current and future needs.

Our Lady Cave became a rare treasure filled with precious memories. Several months after the real wedding took place, Emily and her siblings, Noah and Abigail, enjoyed enacting another wedding with the same bride, groom, preacher, and song. This time, a toy dog was in the audience wearing a pink tutu! I was the photographer, and Gary created an amazing movie using the photos. Our Lady Cave is a multipurpose gem. My dream to create valuable, usable space came true after all—in much better ways than I ever dreamed!

The Mouse, the Trap, and the Bird

The Carolina wren shows up in my life often, sometimes singing its little heart out and other times just relaxing. I may not immediately see the beautiful songbird, but I recognize the familiar chirps that reach my innermost being. A joyful song from the cheerful little bird instantly gets my attention, and I stop what I'm doing to look for the bird. The lyrics my heart hears are "It's all okay, and we're okay." My heart smiles as I enjoy witnessing the beauty of life itself. Sometimes when I hear the bird, I remember when . . .

Catching the elusive mouse at the cabin took months of trying to outsmart it and figure out where it might show up next. I placed the mousetrap where I had seen the most recent droppings, near The Blest Nest's welcome sign next to the front door. Even with yummies such as peanut butter, cheese, and anything else I could think of, I hadn't been able to catch the quiet and sneaky mouse.

As I was eating pistachios during a break from working in the cabin, I wondered if the mouse might be enticed by a pistachio. *T* is for *try*, so I tried. I set the trap, went home for a few days, then started having second thoughts about killing the defenseless mouse. After all, it was just being a mouse. Research led me to create a more humane trap that would lure the mouse into a tunnel with a treat inside. When it found the treat, the weight of the mouse would trip the trap. At that moment, the mouse would fall into an awaiting thirty-two-gallon trash can. My plans were to place the mouse in a smaller container and set it free to live in the woods ten miles away. I had been careful to try to prevent people from killing the spirit of others at The Blest Nest. Unfortunately, my spirit had been crushed on multiple occasions in the past, and I knew what that pain felt like. If anyone at the cabin displayed a bad attitude, they would be asked to leave, and that actually happened a few times. I didn't want to cause pain or hurt anyone intentionally or unintentionally. My heart began to soften toward the mouse. However, the reality was that mice weren't welcome at the cabin. The mouse needed to go elsewhere.

Armed with my newfound knowledge, I was excited when I arrived at the cabin again and could help save the mouse instead of allowing it to be killed by the set trap. As I walked up the steps to the front porch, something was lying on the porch several feet from the mousetrap. There was no mouse in the tripped trap, only the uneaten pistachio. I took a closer look at the still form a few feet away and discovered it was a Carolina wren. It was all my fault the little bird was dead.

Immediately, I began to weep. Thoughts of *if only* pierced my heart, yet what was done was done. *If only I had come yesterday, maybe I could have saved the little bird's life.* This experience brought up thoughts of the abortion and the tragedy of that decision made years ago. It was as if I had been given something tangible to bury that represented Jeremiah's life. I buried the bird under my favorite sparkleberry tree and made a wooden cross from a paint stirrer that we had on-site.

For reasons you can see in the previous paragraph, I call the Carolina wren the *Jeremiah bird*. Now every time I see a Carolina wren, I remember that life is precious and every decision is followed by a consequence, whether it be life-giving or life-taking. Every word that emerges from our hearts and flows through our mouths can either breed life or steal life. Creatures great and small are on this earth for a reason and serve multiple purposes. Learning to observe and listen as they teach is a precious gift. By letting things that bother us go and making the choice to love, we can be agents who breed life. These willful actions can help prevent us from being caught in the grasp of the always-waiting traps.

Good Endings with New Beginnings

7/2/2017, 3:00 a.m.

Several days ago, in the time it took to grab a camera and run back to capture a precious photo, two Carolina wrens had flown away. However, they weren't gone for good. Yesterday, I saw them again, and this time there was a surprise. Two juveniles were in the nest on the eave of our porch. The chirping of their parents, a flurry of activity, and the *peep-peeps* from the little ones alerted me to stand still and witness the beautiful miracle of life through our living room window. The motion picture being recorded in my mind was of great importance, and I didn't want to miss endearing moments to retrieve a camera.

Movement from the mommy bird directed my eyes toward the porch floor to see what the commotion was all about. She was flying to the windowsill, back to the nest, and back to the window—over and over. I peeked through the blinds and saw a down-covered, ready-to-fly fledgling wren sitting on the windowsill, chirp-chirp-chirping in front of me. It was as close to me as it could get, as if to say, "Watch me! I'm learning to fly!"

Within minutes, the family of four had departed. From one perspective, all they left behind was an empty yet meticulously created work of art. However, I was left with more than an empty bird nest. My heart heard God whisper that He would take care of the little birds just as He cares for every living creature, great and small. I witnessed the little one on the windowsill fly away, yet the fluffy little bird reminded me that I am learning to fly too—just in different ways. Empty nests are only empty when we view them that way. Filling up empty nests with soft, sweet, endearing memories can help us keep loved ones near. And if some memories are not so endearing, taking advantage of every moment to create memories worthy of cherishing will add lasting value to our lives.

S O S

2/4/2011

A new order, new way, new reason, new hope, and new birth—God takes care of our needs so well. Many people don't reach out for help, which causes interpersonal relationships and self-esteem to suffer. Either we are too embarrassed by our problems, think nobody will understand, don't know what to do, don't have the resources to get proper treatment, or haven't found the people who can best help us. If I had kept silent about this matter that genuinely matters, I wouldn't have been able to get the help I needed or comfort others in their suffering. Sharing difficulties, struggles, and the painful parts of our lives helps us bring hope to others and gives them the courage to heal.

7/12/2012

Time continues to pass, and things continue to change. I could choose to deny, cry, sigh, or say bye or hi to my physical condition. The health of both my mind and body is determined by the choices I make in each moment. Today, I realized there was a missing part of the team of professionals I've used in the past. The part that was missing is somebody who could actually help me with reaching some sensitive and personal goals. Focusing on my well-being as a whole (physical, mental, emotional, and spiritual) would strengthen my marriage and has already begun to reignite the love Gary and I still have for each other. In loving myself, I have been given enough hope and courage to do what is in our best interest as a couple.

Choosing only to focus on the ultimate destination of pain-free sexual intercourse would not be doing either of us any favors. Being content with where we were each step of the way gave me the opportunity to be mindful, learn important relaxation techniques, get to know how and why my body works the way it does, and learn to work through the pain instead of allowing the pain to work against us. Little successes gave me a much-needed boost in self-esteem. Finding the woman in me was a decision that felt healthy, good, and right.

A different team of professionals was found through The International Pelvic Pain Society's website (pelvicpain.org). I learned that I was not alone, and, calling up my courage and love for myself, I chose to reach out for help. Even though I didn't utilize their services, I decided to tutor myself through available resources online. After reading about the struggles, disappointments, and personal losses of others with a similar condition, I was able to keep on keeping on to find a better garden in which I could grow healthier and stronger in many ways. I pray for healing to enter the lives of others and that, even now, those suffering in silence might see their own pain reflected in my words and reach out for help.

I've come a long way from being the shy little girl I once was, but talking about sexual matters was embarrassing, and I chose to keep these struggles from others. This was not a knee, back, stomach, arm, wrist, heart, lung, leg, foot, or any other part of my body that was easy to discuss. The body, however, is a whole; when something isn't working well in one area, the whole becomes affected. This was a huge mountain for me to climb. I had to put on my big girl pants and keep pressing on, following that star and staying hopeful, no matter how long it took or how far I needed to go.

MAY 2013

Several weeks ago, I received a phone call from a gentleman who wanted to surprise his wife with a stay at the cabin. It was their thirty-sixth wedding anniversary. When I was preparing the cabin for them to enjoy, I was hit with a surprising rush of feelings that didn't surprise God. I had loaded the car, driven an hour, cleaned the cabin spotlessly, and was making up the bed with fresh linens. As I was tucking in the top sheet, a tsunami of emotions overcame me. Without warning, I broke down, fell to my knees beside the bed, and sobbed my aching and pain-ridden heart out. You see, it was also our thirty-sixth wedding anniversary! Back then, I would have never imagined that this was how our marital love life would be.

I prayed hard for our marriage. More specifically, I earnestly prayed that God would restore our sex life, making it better than it had ever been. God knew I meant every word. He knew my heart was broken. My pleas to God for help that day brought the help we needed three years and four months later.

Love is not supposed to hurt, yet sometimes it does. Sex is not supposed to hurt. After delivering three babies in the most common way, my body suffered in uncommon ways. Two back-to-back corrective surgeries were performed when our youngest was eight. Scar tissue set in to further complicate things. Menopause was not my friend and almost did me in. Parts of my body that once had brought me pleasure now had a flashing neon light that illuminated three words—"Do Not Enter." It is interesting how this works. What we want we can't have, and what we can't have becomes the very thing that we want more than anything.

The Lord gave Gary and me reasons to be truly thankful for this long and challenging road we endured. Our sexual sabbatical forced both of us to lean on God as we supported each other. This perceived liability turned into our greatest asset because it brought us as individuals closer to God, which helped us grow closer to each other. Eventually, we became willing to accept whatever outcome we might be left with in the end. Choosing to be content in all circumstances is vital in cultivating joy even while we face afflictions and adversities.

I may never get to see, hear about, or know the ways God will use particular points of pressure I have faced as an individual, wife, and mother. However, I know that my life stories will encourage many by giving hope for healing and relief in similar troubling situations. I have learned there is an art to biting proverbial bullets; a certain amount of skill is needed to bite them while still holding on to grace, dignity, integrity, and respect for others and myself.

When a challenge presents itself in any size, shape, or form, it is worth our time to pay close attention. A good way to respond is to engage in positive and productive actions aimed at the desired result. If one acts with good intentions, the outcome will be wholesome and life-giving and promote a spirit of unity.

Intimacy is an important part of a marital relationship. When that part of a relationship is not good, for whatever reason, mama's not happy, daddy's not happy, and kids can suffer as a result of that displeasure. I chose to go back in time to connect with my sixteen-year-old self, a girl whose innocence was still intact. Gary and I decided to go back to our early days and enjoy dating again. We also worked to recapture the freshness and excitement of our days as newlyweds. Gary continues to be proud of me and tells me so. I thanked him for being so understanding when the out-of-order sign was installed involuntarily. *We can work through this together* became our marital mantra for daily living, no matter what our "this" might be for that day.

> "What shall we say about such wonderful things as these? If God is for us, who can ever be against us?"
>
> —Romans 8:31 NLT

> "Hope deferred makes the heart sick, but a longing fulfilled is a tree of life."
>
> —Proverbs 13:12

SUMMER 2016

I am sixty years old going on a youthful seventeen. My husband is treating me kindly, as a good groom/husband ought. Our painful years as husband and wife are a thing of the past, which makes us grateful for these regifted glory days and, Lord willing, future glory years. Many couples aren't blessed with opportunities for do-overs or marital makeovers. We thank God we worked through our differences, settled disputes in loving ways, and chose to wring out the towel either of us could have thrown in. Our struggles led us to a peaceful shore where we are prepared and able to work with the ebb and flow of life instead of feeling overwhelmed by the cruel, crashing waves that at times will find us all.

It was on Sunday, the seventh day of August; I remember that day well. This particular search-and-rescue mission kept me at the computer all day in my jammies. It was time. I was primed and ready to find someone who could help me instead of inflicting additional hurt either emotionally or physically. Unfortunately, the multiple gynecologists and surgeons I had seen didn't know how to help. Healing, however, doesn't happen according to our schedules. Healing is a process. It cannot be rushed. Being gentle, kind, and loving with myself was important. Healthy, productive seeds had been planted in this freshly cultivated garden. Then I came across an answer on the internet. The mission that originated in the state of Georgia—to locate someone who could restore my body to a functional state—could finally be accomplished, it would seem, in the state of California.

Flying from the East Coast to the West Coast would be a breeze for Sparkles! Mr. and Mrs. Sparkles were hopeful for future possibilities and dreams that were now within our reach. Perseverance and tenacity were my best friends that Sunday. Monday couldn't come soon enough. Our once distant star was reached via phone when the doctor's office opened the next day. A Star Doctor was found within hours of our home by plane!

My quest had been filled with obstacles, yet I never gave up trying and never gave in to feelings of despair. *T* is for *try*. *D* is for *do*. *H* is for *hope*. The answer was found on the other side of The Rocky Mountains. Everything considered—the journey, time, expense, and temporary discomfort—was definitely worth the wait.

"So I say to you, ask, and it will be given to you; seek, and you will find; knock, and it will be opened to you. For everyone who asks receives, and the one who seeks finds, and to the one who knocks, it will be opened."

—Luke 11:9–10 NASB

4/3/2020

I longed for and dreamed about the days I could have a full and passionate romance with my husband, having God's sincerest and highest blessings. With us putting much effort toward this goal, the sky became our limit. The star I aimed for was finally reached after Mr. Sparkles and I landed at LAX in September of 2016 and saw the doctor I had found. In our particular case, SOS was the abbreviation for *Saved Our Sex*. The following information will spell it out for you. I'm smiling just thinking about it!

Who:	Brenda Eller (Patient)
	Dr. David Ghozland (OB-GYN)
What:	The Intimate Renewal™ Procedure
When:	September 21, 2016
Where:	Los Angeles, California
Why:	Because I deserve to be treated like the woman I am.
How:	If interested, please search the procedure's name online.

Thanks, Dr. G! You are a miracle worker, lifesaver, and wife saver, and you became one of the most important puzzle pieces in our marriage. The puzzle pieces now fit together perfectly. You get A+, smiley faces, and countless stars from Gary and me for work well done. Our marriage is being blessed with God's goodness. What was lost is being rebuilt and restored.

I am becoming again instead of just being. My sense of self and womanhood has been revived. Finally, there is validation instead of invalidation and help instead of hurt. I have resurrected my dignity by reclaiming my self-worth. This type of personal achievement has been summed up powerfully as "the ability to have strength and honor despite what has happened in your life and the ability to perpetuate growth, harmony, and peace within yourself and those around you" (WL, my dear friend).

I know that Gary and I haven't been alone in these silent struggles. Please reach out for help if anything in this chapter sounds familiar. Never give up hope. Help may be closer than one believes is possible. Life is too short to give up on our dreams or allow anything to steal our joy. On July 10, 2012, while Gary and I were trying to navigate this challenging road of steep climbs, potholes, and crumbled pieces, I met a compassionate lady named Elizabeth. Although our meeting was brief, eleven words flowed from that angel's heart and held on to me like glue: "God gives people what they need in order to help others."

Fill in the Blank

"Oftentimes, the missing piece doesn't reveal itself until the timing is right."
—Kristyn Mercado

SPRING 2019

My parents were going through years of accumulated things in preparation for a move to another home. Mama called me one day and said, "I just found a puzzle that is missing a piece. The first person I thought of was you. I know Brenda can create the missing piece!" She continued in her soft, sweet, cheerful voice, "You can do it. I know you can!"

I stumbled around trying to come up with reasons why I couldn't do that. I thought, *Is the puzzle really that important to her?* (She wanted to frame it.)

I responded, "We could probably find a replacement puzzle on the internet that would include a perfectly matched substitute for the missing piece."

But she was insistent, so the wheels started turning in my mind.

Daddy told me multiple times while I was growing up—and reminded me after I became an adult—that "can't never could do anything." So I told myself, "I can. Surely, somebody in this world has made a suitable replacement piece for a special puzzle."

I remember a writer's technique I learned in grade school involving the five *W*s and the *H*—asking who, what, when, where, why, and how. "Who" was me, "what" was the puzzle piece, "when" was as soon as possible because I had been striving to be timely with my work, "where" was in my art room, "why" was because Mama deserves to be treated like the queen she is, and the "how" was soon to be discovered.

My search led me to the perfect fit for my puzzle project. I had worked with Sculpey III® oven-bake clay in the past and went to the art store to purchase it and found an appropriate color. *"Buried Treasure"* was a fitting shade because this opportunity was golden, and my creation would become a treasured piece. I proceeded to create a puzzle piece out of Sculpey III that filled in the blank space perfectly. I connected with the treasure that came to life. (The puzzle piece represented blank spaces in my life that were later filled in.) The hardest part of this process was figuring out how to match the coloring and sheen to the connecting pieces so the replacement wouldn't stick out like a sore thumb.

While I was stuck in that dilemma, Mama called me, so excited. "I found it! I found it!" she exclaimed. Safely stored in their china cabinet's drawer was the missing piece. I was relieved to know her puzzle was now whole, and Mama was thrilled.

Being left with a meticulously crafted puzzle piece without a puzzle for it to fit into, I found my creative juices flowing. *This has not been for naught,* I thought. The creation of the puzzle piece inspired the title of this chapter. Then it was up to me to fill in the blank pages with fitting words.

6/3/2019

We can use our imaginations to fill in the blank and attempt to answer the question, "How did my gardens grow?" This becomes uncomfortably personal when this question is asked of oneself. To examine, reflect, and look at oneself honestly—with no restraint—takes courage, humility, vulnerability, and a commitment to care for oneself. Too often, we float through life without paying attention to what is really going on deep inside our hearts and minds. We are too focused on what is before us, around us, and in others to care for ourselves in healthy and loving ways.

Thankfully, God set me on a mission to work on bettering myself. Giving up was not an option. Persevering until I could put difficult chapters of my life to rest brought indescribable peace to my soul. I can move forward in peace because I know this is a new beginning to usher in the best days of my life. I believe that in order for a person to move forward in a better, healthier, and more informed way, they must identify core borers and give them a fitting name. In my life, core borers have been decisions that were made at a time that continued to reinfest hearts and minds years after the unexpected turn of events occurred. Facing my abortion instead of running from it is how the beginning stage of my productive healing process was born.

12/28/2021

This manuscript was rewritten multiple times before I sent it to the editor. On December 4, 2021, I pressed "send," and the manuscript was finally in another person's care instead of mine. That thought makes me want to laugh because more hard work was around the corner. Two days later, I began working in tandem with Mary Beth Bishop, my brilliant editor. The process of revising the manuscript went smoothly as I utilized suggestions from her. It felt easy, as if someone else was doing the thinking for me. I found out quickly, though, that's not the way it works.

Some chapters were harder than others because I needed to fill in the blanks for my readers. It wasn't that the spaces were blank; the message was unclear. I would be alerted to the issue when I came across a word highlighted in yellow. When I clicked on that word, a message from Mary Beth appeared. Many times, I had a deer-in-the-headlights look because that meant something in the text was missing. One time she was wondering what had happened during a particular five-year span I had skated across on purpose. Oh no! Having to dig around inside myself was like cutting open a pumpkin and pulling out all the meat and seeds. Soul surgery hurts!

I learned through this process that deleting the past is impossible. It happened. Erasing mistakes doesn't work; they are written in permanent ink. However, we don't have to let them define us. God forgives every mistake. We must do our part and receive His forgiveness and then forgive ourselves and others.

Thankfully, God forgives abortion. I know that, and I experience His forgiveness every day. However, there were hidden consequences to the decision I made forty-seven years ago in a desperate effort to conceal my sin. One wrong plus one wrong will never equal a right. That was my first pregnancy. I cannot bring Jeremiah back.

Some of those consequences of my decades-old decision came to play in my youngest daughter's life. When our children were in their formative years, Jeff and Erin had parents who were content, happily married, and playful. Kristyn was born when Gary's role at work began to change. The way things were in our household also changed. He was away from home a lot, working at UPS to pay the bills, taking business management classes at school, doing homework, eating, sleeping, and riding his motorcycle. Gary felt neglected and alone because something always seemed to require my time and attention. Caring for three children twenty-four hours a day, seven days a week, taking care of our household, and tending to other responsibilities that fell on me left little time to spend together. It was during that time Gary checked out emotionally. We were no longer the way we used to be as a married couple. I didn't feel loved or validated by him. Real life happened. It hit us hard.

I remember going on field trips with Jeff and Erin. Sitting with them on the bus was fun. They enjoyed me being their chaperone and getting to know their friends. However, it was different with Kristyn. I went on field trips with her also, but she chose to sit in the back of the bus instead of sitting with me. I fought back the tears, but I still showed up because I wanted to be there with her.

The five-year span I referred to earlier needs to be treated with sensitivity and care because details aren't necessary for me to share what is on my heart. Kristyn has been on her pain-filled journey since she was a child. As her mom, I had countless questions: "What did Gary and I do to cause this?" "Where did we go wrong?" "How can we bring her relief instead of grief?" Our lives were complicated, and I was struggling to make sense of it all.

Past traumas had been triggered in me. It was bad. The roots of my abortion were entangled in every part of my life. But I didn't know that until my buried pain began to surface and cry out along with Kristyn's. Meanwhile, I was trying my hardest to push down my pain and silence it through the cloak of denial.

But I wasn't numb anymore. That coping mechanism no longer worked. The focus of my life during those frightening years was keeping Kristyn safe and trying my best to stay sane.

During those years when I was trying to figure out how things had gotten to be the way they were, I made a timeline of events in our family's life that could have easily contributed to her emotional pain. It never occurred to me that the abortion was a core borer in my life. The eggs that my abortion laid had been deposited into my daughter's life in microscopic and unintentional ways.

The reason I feel so strongly about sharing this hard part of my story is that I wish to bring awareness to parents and caregivers of children of any age. Children absorb our stuff. Children carry our baggage. Children feel our wounds and wear our pain unknowingly for years.

I am a perfect example of one who has worked on my issues with authenticity and humbleness. Kristyn is blessed to have a mom who took tender care of her wounds, brought the pain into the light, and shared the story so others can also heal from their pain.

I'm not a therapist, but the following are good morsels to feed the soul . . .

Sometimes, the pain is too deep to think about or share. Digging past the scars can sometimes do more harm than good. Giving someone time, grace, and room to grow at their own pace comforts and helps with their healing process. Revisiting the pits of despair can be depressing and may make things worse. There are times when leaving the past in the past is necessary for the benefit of one's mental, emotional, and spiritual health. Reliving the hard things can be counterproductive and can negatively affect our physical health and relationships. Playing reruns in our mind of *what was*—things we cannot change—steals precious moments we could be embracing and enjoying today.

Letting things go that need to be released is refreshing and brings relief. Focusing on the people in our lives whom we cherish is a healthy way to live in the present. Our futures deserve to be nurtured and respected in the here and now.

Gary, Kristyn, and I are ready to have it all behind us. When we rid ourselves of anything that's unhealthy (that applies to unhealthy thinking), the void needs to be filled with affirming thoughts, healthy habits, true friendships, and anything else that's good and beneficial.

Gary, Kristyn, and I have forgiven each other for the pain we brought into one another's lives. Openness, unconditional love, and forgiveness are vital to healthy relationships. I'm so thankful that Gary and I made the choice to have a third child, that God masterfully wove Kristyn together in my womb, and that Gary and I were chosen to be her forever parents and lifelong friends. She is a treasure and blessing in our lives and a gift to the world.

I happily share the message I received from her on Mother's Day 2020. This mother's dream came true and proves that many prayers have been answered. I love you, Kristyn!

Happy Mother's Day, Mom!

I'm so glad God chose you to be my mother. He knew exactly what He was doing! This is such a special year and a special day to honor you and all the love you've poured out to your family from the very beginning. Since I'm not a mother, I can't understand (at all) the love, grit, pain, joy, energy that it takes. However, I see small glimpses in your book. You are a strong, determined, steady, loving, and joyful mother. You are a fierce protector and encourager. You are transparent and outspoken, and at the same time, lead with a quiet wisdom. Thank you for the many ways you gave and continue to give to your children! I'm so grateful for all that you've taught and are teaching me. The love you give teaches me how to love and give love. I'm very much enjoying getting to learn more about your life's puzzle and all the things that worked together to form you into who you are. You've accepted it all with open eyes, an open heart, and open arms (sometimes after a fight, but still ☺). Your thirst for knowledge, understanding, and meaning is beautiful, and you definitely get all the goody out of life.

I love you,
Kristyn

HeArt Art, Findings, and Broken Things

"He is before all things, and by him all things hold together."

—Colossians 1:17 CSB

5/7/2021

HeArt Art is a form of expression that feeds the soul as the artist uses cast-off items to enhance, create, and bring damaged things to life. Broken things find us, and even as we fix them, they can help us to heal.

I'm not sure when I began picking up discarded items from the ground, but at some point I started cleaning them and creating meaningful and useful art. Flattened, nicely shaped rusted bottle caps turned into backings for beautiful pendants. Unusual pieces of metal have been utilized, and other pieces await their turns to speak wonder into souls. Friends and family have given me jewelry that is no longer useful to them. I pick through and use the jewelry and my "findings" to help create new things. Repurposing these findings gives new life to broken things worthy of restoration. Sometimes patience, glue, love, imagination, and time are all an object needs to become ready to fulfill its purpose.

When our children were still at home and something broke, they would put the item in the Fix-It Shoppe (aka "on the dining room table"). The challenges of restoring item after item were satisfying, not frustrating. People began coming to me with requests to repair special things that had broken, become chipped, needed additional support, or were considered irreparable. They would ask, "Can you bring this back to life?" I would say, "I will do my best and hope for the best." Some things are irreparable and we need to let them go. Yet there are definitely things worth fixing!

Fix-it projects give me a chance to be playful when the broken objects already have personalities. Three porcelain caroler boys were on display every Christmas when I was growing up. Recently, one of them broke, and I was elected to make the redheaded boy stronger, better, and whole. Part of his head was missing.

While he was in the Fix-It Shoppe, my mom was reminded of another piece of hers that was broken. That figurine was of a grandfather and his grandson, whose head was totally missing. I let the two boys meet on our kitchen countertop! It was fun watching the caroler, with his hands behind his back, looking up at his new friend who had no head. He seemed to be saying, "It's okay. She'll make you a new head. She's fixing mine, and it doesn't even hurt!" My mom later found the grandson's head after I made him a new one. Thankfully, the original artist creates faceless figurines!

Breaking Free

I understand fractures and broken bones because I've had a few bad breaks in my lifetime. Our emotional, mental, and spiritual selves can be fractured even though we may not look broken from the outside. However, a fracture is a break that needs time to heal. It is a separation; something has been compromised, and we experience pain.

While looking at a broken antique vase lying on our dining room table in pieces, I visualized parts of my inner life exposed for all the world to see. With intention, I matched each piece to those that best fit together with its uneven shape. Piece by piece, the separated parts received the glue that would hold them together. Strength does come in numbers. The vessel is stronger because of all it went through. Each jagged piece serves a purpose, keeping the vessel securely locked together. Below is an account of the antique vase's journey after I fell in love with it at first sight.

My eyes first met the beautiful vase at an antique store in Hogansville, Georgia. It was purchased to live at The Blest Nest. But after several breaks, I realized its life there was only for a reason and a season. Within seconds of leaving the store with the special antique that had been carefully wrapped for safe travels, I accidentally dropped the bag, and my purchase broke. Even though it wasn't a bad break, I got to know the vessel in a deeper way as I carefully glued the broken pieces together. It grew to be more beautiful in its new state of being.

After the brief visit to Brenda's Fix-It Shoppe, it was time for my special find to move into The Blest Nest. An antique accent table provided support for the vase. Lighted artificial willow branches helped make the restored vessel shine and provided ambient lighting to bless our guests with a homey and pleasant atmosphere. The corner in the breakfast room was an out-of-the-way yet easily seen place for the vase and lights to greet each Blest Nest guest upon arrival. One day, the vase was unintentionally knocked over and shattered upon impact with the floor. Each part of the vessel was gathered up and saved for me. I was thankful to have the pieces, but I knew its useful life at The Blest Nest was over. Our home was where the hand-signed vase needed to live. With gentleness, I restored it to its best incarnation. The vase and artificial willow branches with lights now reside in our new home's breakfast room, providing ambient lighting that makes my heart glow.

Sometimes things have to reach a debilitating state before we are forced to either make positive changes or risk consequences that unaddressed issues will create. In a parallel to real life, the broken vessel reveals a question worth asking: *How many breaks will it take until we are ready to be restored into our best selves?* It may take years to bring us to our breaking points. That's the beautiful part about healing. It will begin when we are strong enough to go through our personal and unique healing journeys.

Hope, solace, joy, and light come when we are placed on our healing path and begin to move forward toward peace. On January 15, 2015, I was purchasing some acrylic paint I needed to make the scars of the vase blend in better with the piece. The cashier approved of the color choices, then she smiled and said, "Good luck! Sometimes the scars make it what it is."

Trash to Treasure

8/6/2011

Work that is done with quality as a goal will result in a product that is special. The extra care implies that the goal was worth the time, effort, and resources expended. The best work we can do is work that we enjoy. Discovering something we are passionate about—and doing that work with giving in mind instead of what we will get out of it—helps us align our activities with who we are as people. It helps better all parts of our being: the mental, emotional, spiritual, and physical.

Certain individuals are able to work under pressure and birth masterpieces; I am not one of them. When I rush the process of art, it sets the stage for carelessness and possibly subpar results. Important parts of the soul of a project could easily get left out, leaving it without a voice.

I used what some people call "mad money" from cleaning other people's homes to purchase furniture and decor for the cabin. The "glad money," as I like to call it, was money well spent. Allowing creative juices and imagination to breathe life into older or broken items was enjoyable, and it saved countless objects from being discarded or regarded as no longer fit for their intended purposes.

When the cabin was in its developmental stage, we had repairs to do at home. Carpenter bees had been using the wooden posts that supported the roof of our porch to deposit their eggs. Replacing the four posts with circular, structurally sound hollow columns made from fiberglass became the perfect solution for our dilemma. Our goal was that the carpenter bees would become bored, frustrated, and depart. After the posts were replaced, they did!

My dad installed the columns but needed to remove a portion from each. As I stacked up the remnants in the basement, I saw what looked like a trash can. Who would have thought that leftovers from our home would become a useful trash can in The Blest Nest? Epoxy paste, fiberglass reinforcement tape, Durham's Rock Hard Water Putty, caulk, oil-based primer, oil-based paint, mosaic tiles, twisted jute string, and an end cap from the HVAC department at our local home-improvement store made the salvaged parts come alive. The components of my trash can treasure had a purpose for being on this planet. Did you know a trash can might have a story to tell? All it might need is a voice.

A talented and sweet friend was helping me design interior portions of the cabin. I had purchased handcrafted rustic decor from her store but suddenly had a new need. Gary and I found a beautiful breakfast room table in another store, but it had no chairs. We bought the table knowing that four chairs would be easy to find. I asked my friend if she had four chairs that might work.

She replied, "I think so! I'll bring them to your house and let you decide." The chairs had come to her minus a table. As it turned out, the table and chairs were a match made in heaven! My friend came to our home that day to *marry* our table and her four chairs.

The chairs were what brought her into an area of our basement where I was storing, creating, and repurposing items for the up-and-coming Blest Nest.

I had been working on creating the trash can, and she was intrigued with the process and wanted to know the story behind my work in progress. After I explained that the four parts represented a person's whole being, with one of them representing the spiritual part, something stirred in her heart. The lamp to her soul was lighted, and she suddenly realized that Jesus was the missing part in her life and in her marriage. She and her husband were already Christians, yet their focus had shifted away from what God wanted in their lives and what they both needed.

After I told her the trash can parable, we went to the backyard and sat on the sturdy rubblestone wall. We enjoyed the serenity of the backyard oasis and talked about the deeper things in life as sisters in Christ. God works in the most mysterious and creative ways!

The Potter's Will

10/18/2010

Were you aware that a coffee mug can dance? Mine danced solo for the first time this morning! Yesterday, I attended the Hogansville Hummingbird Festival. The beauty of pottery fascinates me, and I searched every pottery booth at the festival for pieces that might tug on my heartstrings. Every work of art at Sherie Spain's booth was unique and captivating. Sherie was approachable and friendly. I knew she had to be proud of her meticulously formed creations. Each piece caught my eye, and I wondered if I would ever be able to master the art of ceramics.

My heart must have been melting into each piece because Sherie saw two focused eyes sparkling with passion. The flood of questions from me was welcomed by ready answers: *yes,* she was a teacher, and, *no,* she was not too far away for me to be trained by her. As it is with every purpose under heaven, there will be a time, season, and reason for me to enter that training field if it's meant to be. Sherie understood that I wouldn't be able to begin classes immediately since I'm focused on bringing this book to fruition.

After I told her about the book, her eyes searched one of her tables. Then Sherie asked *me* a question: "Do you like to drink coffee?" My automatic affirmative nod was understood. She then picked up a beautiful coffee mug, removed the price tag, and said, "Here. You can think of me as you write your book."

My heart had been won and the depths of my soul were warmed by the impressive memories of yesterday. I had been looking forward to waking up this morning so I could try out my elegant coffee mug that will be treasured forever. Before I turned in for the night, I turned on the coffee pot and brewed a full pot of coffee for the early risers to enjoy. As I did so, this night owl came to a screeching halt at the coffee pot. Another beautiful memory had been made that day. It was a promise Sherie made to me that I will share at the end of this chapter.

This morning, as the dawn turned into day, I remembered the special coffee mug that awaited its first cup of hot coffee. Since the coffee was cold, it needed a little help to satisfy the end user. The beautiful coffee mug began its useful life at 7:25 a.m., October 18, 2010. It seemed to take on a life of its own in our microwave. When the door was shut, buttons had been pushed, and the light came on, the mug slowly twirled round and round as if it were back on the potter's wheel. This time, however, it was about to begin its useful life in the spotlight as a blessing. The touch of the potter's loving hands had clearly left its mark as I imagined Sherie creating the work of art that was gracefully dancing with delight before me.

Sherie became a master potter because she maintained her focus, practiced, never gave up, made herself available to learn, and did what it took (and more) to be successful. Now, she experiences the satisfaction and joy of teaching, training, and blessing others.

During my visit with Sherie at her booth, I asked if she could make two vessel sinks for the cabin. Even though she had never made a sink, Sherie took on the challenge. We planned to meet at the cabin, where templates could be made for her custom-size creations. This would also give her a chance to get a feel for the setting her sinks would be a part of. Before I left Sherie's booth at the festival, I gave her ideas about what I wanted one of the sinks (which would represent me) to look like. Knowing I couldn't choose them all, I picked over the smorgasbord of ideas, colors, and designs she had used in her pieces on display, then selected those that were irresistible. She wrote as I spoke, taking notes on what was important and meaningful to me.

The trip from her home in Alabama to the cabin proved to be beneficial for Sherie. Before she headed back, I watched her gather oak leaves to use as imprints in the clay and huge acorns so she could replicate the real thing. I gave Sherie the freedom to "make a free-form bowl with a hole," and I would take care of creating a level base and making the hole larger to fit the drain. I wasn't specific with the colors and design for the second sink. I just said, "Surprise me! I'm sure whatever you create will be beautiful."

11/4/2011

Sherie left me a voicemail last night at 6:09 p.m. to let me know she had just finished the first vessel sink that was created for The Blest Nest's master bathroom. "Hey, this is Sherie Spain. I'm just calling to give a report about your new sink. It's probably the prettiest thing I've ever made in my life. I put leaves all over it and acorns on it and embedded leaves in the sink. It's absolutely gorgeous! I was so excited I just had to call and tell you. Everybody around here is oohing and ahhing over it. People from other places are walking in and saying, 'I've heard about the sink. I've gotta come see it.' Bye!"

Today, Sherie explained that the sink had not been glazed or put in the kiln for firing. That part of the process should take about two weeks. She said, "I just hope it doesn't break." I felt confident it would survive the heat and come out stronger on the other side.

10/16/2013

Both vessel sinks made it through the firing process without breaking. Sherie went beyond the call of duty and aimed to please. I knew she would deliver on her promise without a doubt. Sherie could tell that I was partial to the first sink because it represented my life. She created the sink to sparkle, shine, and speak. Her hard work and efforts paid off. Everything Sherie did to "will the sinks into being" is deeply appreciated.

Our Blest Nest guests felt special and pampered at the cabin. The vessel sinks played an important part in making that a reality. Linda, the Blest Nest guest you met at the beginning of this book, shared these words in the cabin's guest book: "I enjoyed the poetic sayings and spiritual truths all through The Blest Nest. I have several items that made me happy, the lighted trees and the lighted porch swing. But my most favorite was the basin in the bathroom. The way the water ran reminded me of my granddad's water pump. The color and the design were so beautiful!"

Job well done, Sherie! When I grow up, I want to be like you.

I may not be a potter,
I may not learn those skills.
Yet I have told the Potter,
"Use me, Lord. Do your will."

Brenda Eller

Spring with Autumn in Winter

WINTER 2017

Fertile ground has been cultivated and is ready for new seeds to grow in a stronger and more productive way. A new way of looking at life, things, and people has left me with a sparkle of hope, a sprinkle of cheer, and a peace that is so pure and rich it is indescribable. The last five years have been hard and were filled with difficult relationships that left me feeling spent. It is liberating that people who caused so much havoc are out of my life for good. I had to dig my way out of the aftermath, dust myself off, and regain my composure. It was only by the grace of God that I came out on top of that mountain. God always follows through on His promises with protection, love, and provision.

On a recent visit to surprise our grandson Eli on his fifth birthday, Gary and I took goodies to share with him and his preschool friends. We were warmly welcomed by all. There was one little girl who confidently walked up to me and said, "Hi! My name is Autumn, and I'm five years old." Something about Autumn enchanted me, although I couldn't put my finger on it . . . not yet.

The goodies were served and enjoyed, then Gary read a book to the class. His captive audience was fully engaged as they sat on the floor interacting with him. After the story time, I was asked to sit with Gary at the front of the room while the children rehearsed a Christmas presentation we would have otherwise missed. We felt honored and were being blessed in multiple ways. When the rehearsal was over and we were still seated, multiple children surrounded us in a group hug.

The children then began lining up for recess, and the room grew quiet. Autumn walked toward me with an outstretched hand, and within the clasp of her finger and thumb, I saw a shiny gold sequin. She smiled and said, "Here is a sparkle for you!"

My heart melted. How did she know to use the word *sparkle* and then give me one?

The teacher witnessed the sweet gift exchange from Autumn's heart to mine. She said, "Autumn enjoys finding things on the ground."

That was it! Autumn and I are kindred spirits. We both enjoy finding things on the ground and using them to bless others. That sparkle made its way onto my "Sparkles necklace," which had been given to me as an early Christmas gift. It's amazing how one tiny sequin can become so inspiring. Going a step further, it's miraculous how individuals can be inspired to give what they give when they give without knowing how far their gift may reach, what part of the gift will touch the heart of another, or what conversations will be birthed from the seeds planted through the kindness of caring souls.

Unusual objects have their places in our lives and can teach us valuable real-life lessons. For instance, I was once given a beautiful necklace with multiple pendants and a special charm. However, once I put the necklace on, I noticed that one of the pendants was weighty and unbalanced, causing the entire necklace to twist in bothersome and unbecoming ways. The only way to fix the necklace so I could enjoy wearing it was to remove the problematic part and redesign the necklace so that the pieces would be well matched.

Personalizing the necklace was a similar process to the way we must change things around a bit when something in our lives isn't working. We must reassess, reconfigure, and reincorporate into our lives that which works and allows pleasantness to abound. The sparkle from my new little friend named Autumn reminds me that every gift (no matter how small) has significance and worth, just like every human being does. No matter how bad our problems might be, spreading the tiniest seeds of kindness will bring growth.

During recess with Eli and his classmates, I watched the children as they interacted with one another. Autumn found a thin piece of ice floating in a small water puddle. As she held up the special find for me to see, one of the boys walked by, took the ice out of her hand, looked at me and kept walking as if to ask, "What are you going to do about it?" As a witness to the incident, I thought it best to choose my battles, redirect, and let it go. Thankfully, Autumn did the same.

In my quest to have fun and play with the children, I said, "Hey, Autumn, come here. I know you're good at finding things on the ground. Let's find some ice. I'm sure we can find more around here somewhere." She eagerly began looking for ice with me. Both of us spotted four small pieces of ice at the same time. Autumn found three friends to help her bury the ice in a sandpit. Our special mission had been accomplished, and she happily played with friends who were being friends with her.

I thought of the boy who *stole* the ice from Autumn. The ice in his hand would soon have melted and evaporated as if it had never been there. What he thought he had, he lost. Greediness, using people, and taking advantage of others (just because they're there) eventually will hurt the taker the most. I chose to take the higher road with the boy; sometimes it's best just to let things go.

When we innocently hold our sparkle out for the world to see, someone may walk up to us like that boy did to Autumn and take it from us just because they can. During my lifetime, I've allowed people to steal my joy, wipe the smile off my face, and stomp on my heart. When I decided to stand up for myself instead of allowing others to take advantage and use me for their benefit, things began to change. Letting go of those people was necessary for my well-being.

Little sparkles of spring during winter-weary days lighten and brighten this world with joy and delight.

12/19/2017

Kristyn shared book-worthy comments with me after reading this chapter:

You speak words of truth, freedom, and wisdom. I experience you as so completely centered in truth, self, and source (things I'm working on) and as a loving and living example to others to do the same. The older and wiser you get, the more unbreakable, unshakeable, and beautiful you become!

I'm thinking of "How is my garden growing?" because it's a process that will never end. You speak to the most important part of creating a clear, clean, fertile, and willing foundation from which all things good, beautiful, and pure can begin, flourish, and spread. Wow. I'm deeply inspired by you!

I love you dearly and am so grateful to have you as my mom—a strong woman who is committed to truth and love! You are such a gift to me and the world. Thank you for having the courage to keep stepping into love in so many ways.

Writing: HeArt Art

2/9/2021, 3:44 a.m.

Putting this manuscript together for better has been, is, and will be challenging, educational, and motivating. It makes me appreciate every author behind every word in every book in addition to every person who helped each writer bring their baby to life. This book will grow wings of its own, find its way into hearts, and land where it will nest best. Expressing important ideas and feelings in creative ways is art. Art speaks best when it comes from the heart.

HeArt Art comes from the deepest recesses of one's being. From the garden planted in the soul, works arise to comfort, bless, and regenerate our world. The cover design for this book is a perfect example of HeArt Art. Since you are reading this chapter, it can be assumed that you learned about my love for the Carolina wren while reading the chapter called "The Mouse, the Trap, and the Bird." Also, you may have wondered what the buried-treasure puzzle piece looked like after reading the "Fill in the Blank" chapter.

Designing this book's cover led me down a new path of discovery and awe. This important work was best left to a professional. I was enthusiastically referred to Roy Appalsamy at AMDesign Inc. in Canada. My main desire for the cover art was that the wren and the puzzle piece be included. Roy took it from there, and I'm amazed and pleased with his work. He knew the wren and puzzle piece were important to me, and he requested a photo of the puzzle piece. Gary was the photographer; I was his assistant. The puzzle piece on the cover is an undoctored photo of the now-revealed *buried treasure.*

Lavender crocus blooms add special interest and intrigue to the book's cover. Roy surprised me with them! Crocuses in every stage of development are symbols of hope that fit well with the manuscript's message. The flower emerges when we need it to refresh our winter-weary gardens and reminds us that spring will come again soon. Hannah Flagg Gould (1789–1865) eloquently captured thoughts from a crocus in her poem "The Crocus's Soliloquy." Her poem ends with words of hope from a flower:

Many, perhaps, from so simple a flower
This little lesson may borrow—
Patient to-day, through its gloomiest hour,
We come out the brighter to-morrow![20]

The Greater-Good Garden

God's plans for me are much greater than anything I could have ever come up with on my own. Is God still good when His answer is "no"? Yes, he is. Sometimes we have to let go of our plans to take hold of God's purpose.[21]

—Sharon Jaynes

3/29/2020, 9:00 a.m.

The world as we know it is changing as of this writing. The coronavirus pandemic (COVID-19) has our world in its grip, and no one knows when it can be contained, controlled, or eradicated. Viruses live on hosts; thousands of humans all over the world have contracted the virus, and thousands have lost their lives and loved ones. The number of cases rises at an alarming rate each day.

I put myself in lockdown and have not left our newly purchased home in weeks. The timing for putting this book together was perfect, yet my heart breaks over all the suffering, loss, and hardships COVID-19 has created and will create. This enemy is invisible to the naked eye, yet the symptoms and aftermath can be clearly seen and experienced and will be felt for many years to come.

Courageous and generous people have come out of the woodwork to do anything they can to help. The heroic efforts of layers and layers of people are touching and inspire me to do more. I'm so grateful for healthcare workers, first responders, grocery store workers, teachers, and other professionals on the front lines. We all thank you for the sacrifices you and your families have made and will make.

As I walked up the stairs carrying a fresh cup of coffee, I knew I was entering a field that was ripe for harvest. God provided me with the perfect set-apart space, along with time, for putting life puzzles together for better. Sparkles' Sanctuary is the name I gave the bonus room in our new home. Gary gave me his blessing to use the room for myself in any way that worked best. With a full bath, walk-in closet, central heating, and air-conditioning, I had all I needed.

The existing robin-egg-blue walls were perfect; I didn't change a thing. A shower curtain with a picture of a huge anchor was left by the previous owner. This reminds me that we understand the value of the anchor when we feel the storm. Hebrews 6:19 tells us, "We have this hope as an anchor for the soul, firm and secure."

Another Bankers Box was waiting for me on the table that is painted with a sunflower design in "My Tent of Meeting" (the name I chose for the eight-man log-cabin tent in Sparkles' Sanctuary). I purchased the tent when we lived at our former home because I wanted to have a special place to think and write, a "she shed" of sorts. Because of zoning ordinances, we were unable to build a permanent special place in the backyard oasis because it would have been too close to the creek. Over time, I realized setting up and taking down the tent in the backyard would not serve me well long term. When we moved to our new home, and Gary gave me his blessing to use the bonus room in any way that worked best, I remembered my tent that had never been used. Gary set it up for me in Sparkles' Sanctuary, and it nested in the far side of the room perfectly. It's out of the weather and has a screen-mesh roof. The writing desk from Our Lady Cave is always ready for me on the tent's screened-in porch. The sign on the wall in Sparkles' Sanctuary says it best: "Welcome Home." Yes, God provided everything I needed and more.

I was ready to, once again, go through the boxes of raw material and separate chaff from the proverbial *edible* grain. The results of the winnowing process would be well worth the time spent in an intensive yet quiet search-and-rescue mission to gather God-given treasures for this book. One of the precious finds is a poem written on October 19, 2011, the day after I knew a sabbatical was needed during that season in my life. It is titled "20/20." I believe it to also be applicable to this sabbatical season in the year 2020.

This is the year to go through words. You've written adjectives and verbs.
The people, places, and hard things connect each dot. Plumb lines I'll bring.
Watch fears you had of yesteryear miraculously disappear.
You'll rise to be a better you. My Light will shine through all you do.
Enjoy your days, my special child. Remember Me; be meek, be mild.
Stay close to Me; I am your friend. I'll help you nail down each loose end.

I love you,
The Master Carpenter

3/30/2020, 6:42 a.m.
I woke up this morning eager to put "The Greater-Good Garden" chapter together. Parts and pieces of the chapter's message were in a gallon-size clear zippered bag. We can try to see through something that's not fully clear, yet know somewhere in the recesses of our hearts, minds, spirits, bodies, and souls that change and clarity are needed. When it becomes clear what we ought to do, it is better to fumigate any bitter critters and core borers that have been renting space in our minds and enjoying their unnerving campouts in our hearts.

Better Bugs gain the victory over bitter critters and core borers. I coined these three names because they remind me of the behavior of human beings. It's good to set beneficial bugs loose in a vegetable garden because they help protect the plants from insects that cause damage. I discovered a creative and enjoyable way I can think outside the box and allow Better Bugs to come in and help. One of the papers in the bag was carefully chosen and examined. It is titled "Better Bugs." I adopted one of the words from the "Better Bugs" list to utilize every day of this year and every gifted day afterward. It is the action word *forgive*. I needed to dig in and find help to do forgiveness well. Two additional words on the list begin with *F*; they are *family* and *friendship*. Choosing to embrace these value-packed words every day will help make life better no matter what gets served on the plate of the day. Helping keep bitter critters and core borers from infesting and causing damage within and without is well worth the personal investment. In utilizing the three words together, our individual selves, homes, relationships, and the world will be a better place in which to live.

One doesn't have to focus only on one, two, or three of the words on the list. They can all be born within if they are not already there. It is a choice that begins in the mind, attaches to the heart, and blooms as we become better on both the inside and the outside. This challenge is well worth considering because it will benefit our communities as a whole.

3/9/2021

Today, Corrie Gerbatz posted a wisdom-filled entry on the Proverbs 31 Ministries website (proverbs31.org) titled "When We Feel Beyond Help." She shared insights that can help many people going through various trials, and she included this pointed message: "May we never lose sight of God's grace-filled streams always at work in our lives, carving a path in our hearts."[22] After reading Corrie's wonderful post, I scrolled through the comments from her readers. A relatable comment from Shirlee Abbott jumped out of the computer and gave me a heartfelt hug. Based on the words in Corrie's post and Shirlee's timely comment, I could tell that they understand the challenges that parenting presents. They also know that God is always there to help us *when we feel beyond help*. Shirlee's welcomed comment would have been helpful for Gary and me while we were being "raised" by our God-given children.

Shirlee wrote, "I, too, was that mama 'who clearly needed a timeout of her own.' I didn't know it back when I was the mother of teens with attitudes, the times I should have put myself in the corner—my prayer corner. To all the moms frustrated by endless battles with stubborn teens, I say: You're not in a battle WITH your child; you're in a battle FOR your child. Send them to their rooms less; head to your prayer room more. Speak fewer words of criticism and more words of blessing. Listen to their anger in love, the way God listens to your anger. Think discipline, not punishment. Pray less for compliance in the moment and more for the godly adult you want the child to become."[23]

Greater-Good Gardens grow when we focus on anything that helps us bring about harmony within ourselves, our families and friendships, and communities at large. Choosing the seeds we plant with concern for the bigger picture instead of what we will personally gain in the moment requires sacrifice coupled with obedience to do the just, fair, and right thing. Life is filled with parts and pieces that don't make sense. Being a bigger person by giving others and ourselves opportunities to grow through support, encouragement, and a whole lot of love will give each seed the best possible environment in which to grow. Greater-Good Gardens provide safe places to heal, grow, and thrive.

9/12/2021

I entered a true and established Greater-Good Garden on multiple occasions as an infant, child, and teenager. During every visit, I was unaware of the amazing gifts I was being given. Leila Daughtry-Denmark, M.D., was my pediatrician and doctor until I graduated from high school. No matter how old I was at the time, she never seemed to change. Her long gray hair was neatly tucked into a bun, her white doctor's jacket and dress were clean and pressed, and her caring eyes sparkled. I remember her whistling like a bird when she checked my ears (when I was a little kid). When Dr. Denmark was ready for the next patient, she opened the waiting room door and asked, "All right, who's the next angel?"

Dr. Denmark's clinic was part of her home so she could be close to her family. She didn't make appointments, and a sign-in sheet welcomed her patients in the waiting room. My mom recalls what it was like to have Dr. Denmark on her side to help take care of the three Surles' girls in the best way possible. She remembers Dr. Denmark as being down to earth and having a huge heart for people, especially the children. Parents of growing children were taught ways to help the children learn to do things for themselves and to care for others by showing love.

During our visits, she made us feel valued and special. We appreciated her ability to do all we saw her do and more, even though we never fully knew what "more" entailed. I could sense the trust my mom felt, and that helped me know I could trust her too. It was comforting to be under her care. Dr. Denmark was accurate, reliable, thoughtful, and kind. She had a caring way about her and wouldn't let anything go undone or unaddressed. Taking care of things in a calm way when issues came up was admirable. Her sense of humor helped. And when we needed to go see Dr. Denmark, lunches were packed because we would end up staying half the day to wait our turn. The doctor visits were enjoyable, and decades later, Dr. Denmark still brings to mind precious memories.

The Lord blessed Dr. Denmark with a long, fulfilling life, parts of which are documented on her official website (drleiladenmark.com). Extensive information about her life and amazing contributions to this world can be found there. On May 31, 2019, a video was produced by WXIA-TV titled *Preserving history: the legacy of Dr. Leila Denmark*. During the video, her daughter Mary Denmark Hutcherson shared, "My mother helped develop whooping cough vaccine. This was, I think, one of the important things that she was involved with in her lifetime, was working on something that would save the lives of children and adults."[24]

Little did we know at the time that my sisters and I were part of history in the making as we were being nurtured, taught, loved, and cared for by such a remarkable and legendary doctor and person. Dr. Denmark was doing what she loved; it wasn't work. Forsyth County News published an article on July 29, 2018, headlined "Legacy of Dr. Denmark lives on through new school."[25] Kelly Whitmire wrote:

> In the early 1970s, Denmark wrote a book of her views of childcare titled *Every Child Should Have a Chance*[26] and would give a little piece of advice when she autographed the book.
>
> "Then she would write, 'Do what you can do to help,' and underlined it," Mary Hutcherson said, "directing it to the people that would be raising children."

Dr. Denmark dedicated her book "To the Giver of Life and those who help to preserve it." Seeds that were planted in the hearts and lives of those she helped and taught continue to grow and multiply many years later. Each seed was nurtured with love, sacrifice, obedience, care, and devotion to a great cause, making this world a kinder, healthier, and more loving place. I dedicate "The Greater-Good Garden" chapter to Dr. Denmark's memory and legacy. Thank you, Dr. Denmark, from the depths of my heart.

Leila Alice Daughtry-Denmark, M.D.
February 1, 1898–April 1, 2012

By touching one heart at a time and planting one seed at a time, we can help keep this true angel's Greater-Good Garden growing, thriving, and multiplying. I can hear Dr. Denmark's voice echoing in my ear as I imagine her opening the door to the waiting room and asking, "All right, who's the next angel?" Then the message rings clear enough for me to hear so my heart can understand her words: "Every child should have a chance. Do what you can do to help."

Better Bugs

Achievement	Generosity	Opportunity
Appreciation	Get Along	Optimism
Being There	Good Examples	Parenting
Believe	Good Manners	Patience
Believe in Yourself	Gratitude	Please and Thank You
Caring	Hard Work	Reaching Out
Character	Helping Others	Resilience
Civility	Honesty	Respect
Commitment	Hope	Right Choices
Compassion	Imagine	Sharing
Compliments	Including Others	Sportsmanship
Confidence	Inspiration	Spread Your Wings
Courage	Integrity	Strength
Courtesy	Kindness	Teaching by Example
Determination	Listening	True Beauty
Devotion	Live Life	Wonder
Do Your Part	Live Your Dreams	
Encouragement	Love	
Endure	Loyalty	
Family	Making a Difference	
Forgive	Mercy	
Friendship		

Toxicity to Tonicity

4/23/2013

Mental toning is a form of tonicity and helps strengthen a person's ability to bounce back with vigor after being sideswiped emotionally by another person. Curiosity compels me to search for answers as I did when I asked myself, *Where do seeds of jealousy come from? Is there a preemergent we can spray on those seeds to keep them from germinating in people?* Toxic vapors are emitted from those who are feeling secondary emotions. Those vapors, in turn, seep into places in the hearts of those who, more than likely, need to heal hurts from their past. Secondary emotions are similar to secondary infections. They let us know that one ailment has grown into something more. When something a person says or does makes another person feel inadequate, deficient, less than, or left out, hurt feelings may come out in unpleasant and unbecoming ways, directed toward the real or perceived offender(s). A person who doesn't accept and love him or herself just as they are finds it hard to be genuinely happy for another person's success—and even harder to accept and love the other person just as they are.

A visiting preacher was at a church Gary and I recently visited. Scott Wozniak's sermon was titled "Insecurity Is at the Root of All Sorts of Evil." I wholeheartedly agree with the preacher's observation. The love of money and all types of insecurities can drive people to say and do the darndest things. Toxic people, however, can be our star teachers if we allow ourselves to be taught. The hardest teachers in our lives are the ones who push us until we hurt enough, stretch enough, and learn enough. They may not realize they are sprinkling raindrops on us all day long for weeks, months, or years on end. Toxic people may not know that their words, looks, and unbecoming behaviors won't leave us alone as we go about our daily lives. I learned that unbecoming behaviors of others can help us grow if we're open to view them that way.

What do we do with the toxic people in our lives when we feel obligated to be around them because of family ties or mutual close friendships? How can we stop getting caught up in their sick, senseless games when we become aware of what's been going on? First and foremost, it's best to look deeply within and change what we can change about ourselves. We are incapable of making others change to suit our expectations, needs, and wants, just as they are incapable of making us fit into molds of their choosing. It could be possible that we ourselves are unknowingly depositing toxic "draindrops" into the life of another.

Considering the interests of others above our own can help us change our positions, relax our stances, look at ourselves from other people's perspectives, and possibly come to understand their points of view. We cannot fully know where they've been in life or where they are now, and they cannot know all there is to know about us. It's impossible to know for certain what's fueling their thinking, and it's impossible for them to know for certain what's feeding ours. Those things we all have in common.

The next step sounds so simple, quick, and easy, yet it's one of the most difficult steps I've had to take. It brought about good outcomes, though. Take a step in the right direction and bless the difficult ones as you release them from your life. At that liberating moment in time, we are releasing ourselves from the control we have let them have over us. This one step is so monumental and powerful that it breaks through the mountain, creating a tunnel that protects us and gets us to the other side in a better way. God's Word tells us to "bless those who curse you, pray for those who mistreat you" (Luke 6:28). Deep-seated ill will miraculously turns into goodwill when the ways of God are implemented and we are fully engaged, willing to do what God asks of us with sincere hearts and pure motives. He will be pleased when we do our part, pray, and leave the outcomes to Him.

Blessing those who have hurt us deeply releases them into God's care in one empowering step. We can thank God, knowing the best thing for all involved was done. People will throw their pain out into the world because they don't know what to do with it. However, we do not have to be active participants by holding on to their pain. Let the other person be, pray for them, and love without conditions. Take care of yourself. And love yourself. Release anything that keeps you unbalanced, stuck, and ineffective. A well-balanced life doesn't just happen; one must strive to reach their best level of tonicity.

"BE" ATTITUDES

Being
Empowered

Activates
Triumphant
Thinking
Inspiring
True
Understanding
Deemed
Essential for
Success

Success is not about money. To me, success is being able to lay my head down at night knowing that honesty was honored, respect was respected, truth was told, love was lived, and lives were changed. A sage lady named Elaine once told me, "There is no amount of money that can compensate for quality of life."

LOVE NEVER FAILS

1/6/2009

Loving
Others
Varying
Energies

Necessitates
Embracing
Volatility
Every day
Rendering

Forgiveness
Acceptance
Inspiration
Love without conditions
Selflessness

B IS FOR BLESS

4/16/2010, 1:20 a.m.

Bless those who seem like enemies, bless those who truly are.
Bless those who make it hard to love, bless those close and afar.
"God, help me! This one's hard to do—much easier said than done.
I cannot bless without You here. My God, to You I come.

How ought I act toward that one when I've been antagonized?
How ought I act when I've been wronged, unjustly criticized?
How ought I act when grace gets lost? They shared their curse with me.
Can I bring out best dishes? Have a big pity party?"

"Love 'em anyway," I've heard. I chose to love, not pout.
It worked when I changed thinking and let God work tough things out.
Although I did not understand, I tried the best I could.
I found that pity grew in me to forgive them as I should.

Dissension, discord, differences—disputes trip us, then bind.
We think thoughts that we ought not think, then thoughts get thrown from minds.
With the attitude of a peacemaker, God says we will be blessed.
We can enjoy great happiness—on Earth, find Heaven's bliss.

God says we will be comforted. Choose peace and then pursue.
Pray for the ones on every side of life. May God bless you.

Brenda Eller

TREES

The point is not who's right or wrong.
Important is that relations be strong.
Wearing chips on our shoulders is not healthy.
If we zoom in closer, we'll see self's tree.

The chips on our shoulders feel like heavy boulders;
They fell from self's tree as the heart grew colder.
The people we love are people like us;
When they make mistakes, we begin to fuss.

Forgiveness and grace are what we should give,
For this is the way God taught us to live.
He gave us these gifts to give for free . . .
Great example to help us get rid of our trees.

When self's tree is gone, we suddenly see
That others are not as we saw them to be.
Our hearts and lives then unite as one
To show us true peace and rest has come.

Brenda Eller
11/6/2008

New Season: Part One

Gary's Story

3/28/2020

We don't often use the word *covenant* in conversation. Most of us have little understanding of the word. When we think of marriage, we usually do so in terms of a contract rather than a covenant. In reality, the two words are quite different. The difference is what held our marriage together.

Basically, a contract is an agreement between two or more persons signifying that all signing parties will do something. Legally, marriage is a contract with certain rights and responsibilities, but it is important to distinguish between legal marriage and covenant marriage. In a legal marriage, if one party doesn't live up to a contract, then legal actions force him or her to do so or to end the marriage with an equitable settlement. Society couldn't exist without laws regulating marriage relationships. So in this sense, marriage is a contract. However, marriage, as intended by God, is more than this; it's a covenant.

Covenant is used many times in the Bible to describe God's relationship with humans. In each case, a covenant represents a very serious decision and is sealed with a commitment that nothing can end the agreement except death. When two people stand before God, family, and friends and state that they will remain married *for better or worse, till death do us part,* they are making a covenant and not a contract. Marriage is an earthly example of God's covenant with humans. When two people enter into a covenant relationship, they are entering into a commitment that they will meet every challenge together and never quit.

The problem arises when you view your marriage only as a contract or as a series of contracts. When this happens, you will leave the door open to allow you to walk away at any time. The Bible views marriage ultimately as a covenant, although contracts may be an important part of carrying out your covenant. Please take a minute and review the characteristics of each below.

There are four general characteristics of contracts:

1. Contracts are often made for a limited period of time.

    Although most marriage ceremonies involve the phrase, *"till death do us part,"* many couples interpret that as "We're committed to each other as long as this relationship is mutually beneficial."

2. Contracts often deal with specific actions.

    Most informal contracts made within the marriage also deal with specific actions. Such informal agreements can be a positive way of living out a covenant marriage.

3. Contracts are based on an if-then approach.

    This mentality could lead one spouse to rely on the other for happiness. If so, the couple could struggle deeply in the first several years of their marriage.

4. Contracts are created because of a desire to get something.

    People sign a lease because they want to have a car. The salesman signs the contract because he wants the commission. Many conversations in marriage are initiated because the husband or the wife are motivated to get something.

Covenant Characteristics

A covenant, like a contract, is an agreement between two or more persons, but the nature of the agreement is different. The biblical pattern reveals five characteristics of covenants.

1. Covenants are initiated for the benefit of the other person.

    Many of us can honestly say that we entered marriage motivated by a deep desire to benefit the person we were about to marry. Our intention was to make them happy. However, when needs aren't met, spouses can revert to a contract mentality.

2. In covenant relationships, people make unconditional promises.

    Covenant marriages are characterized by unconditional promises, such as those spoken during traditional wedding vows.

3. Covenant relationships are based on steadfast love.

    In a marriage, steadfast love refuses to focus on the negative aspects of one's spouse. Steadfast love is a choice.

4. In covenant relationships, commitments are viewed as permanent.

    As Christians, we must not lower the ideal. This standard can only be attained if we live out the fifth distinguishing element of covenants.

5. Covenant relationships require confrontation and forgiveness.

These two responses are essential in a covenant marriage. *Confrontation* means holding the other person responsible for his or her actions. *Forgiving* means a willingness to lift the penalty and continue on in a loving, growing relationship. Ignoring the failures of your spouse isn't the road to marital growth.

Covenant marriage is God's plan, and it is the covenant that Brenda and I made that kept us together *for better or worse*, and there were a lot of both.

People Don't Stay the Same

I have learned a lot about myself and my amazing wife. The most important thing that I have learned is that all people change. Neither you nor the person you marry stay the same. The beauty of marriage is that the covenant union becomes a safe place for two people to evolve. Years flew by before I understood this vital truth.

At one point, we were both happy, with few cares in this world and free to enjoy each other. You already know much about our marriage since Brenda has provided many details of our lives together in this book. I will simply state that the most difficult lesson I learned was that life was not all about me.

Life drastically changed when I decided to exchange my wonderful truck-driving job for a management position to gain the approval of others. A key point to note here is that my identity was unclear. Rather than accepting my true identity—who God says I am—I foolishly followed the expectations of others as my identity. It was at that point that Brenda and I began to experience the separation of our paths as I began my journey into a foreign world. The hours of solitude and meditation disappeared, and so did I. As I look back, many good things resulted from my journey; however, the journey came with a price.

Job promotions, along with the completion of my undergraduate and master's degrees, left little time for pleasure and contemplation. My schedule had me working around the clock, and I was often on the job at night. Sleeping in a camping trailer in the front yard with a fan during the day to find some peace and quiet was not my idea of happiness. There was nowhere else to go. I needed to provide for a wife and three children, and my purpose became survival.

Brenda raised the children and managed the home, and I was present as much as I could be. And all the while, Brenda and I silently grew further apart. I will be vulnerable here, probably to the point of being uncomfortable. Intimacy was an important part of my vision for marriage. With all that was going on, time together was scarce. Understanding that women change physically was a tough lesson. Without going into too much detail, I will simply say that after giving birth to three children, Brenda was no longer able to have sexual intercourse. For the next twenty years, the blissful early days of marriage seemed to be a distant memory. The way we had been then was gone.

An additional surprising factor in our issues came with the mental changes that occurred with age. As we were no longer a young couple but headed toward sixty-something, the question of "What do we do with our short lives?" became more frequent. Questions about our future, accompanied by differences in visions and goals, began to unravel our once-wonderful marriage. We knew we were in trouble, and we were committed to seeking the help of counselors and friends. Our church was aware and prayed, as we did, that we would somehow survive the years of desolation. The bottom line is this: we can choose to enjoy or choose to destroy.

Time goes on, and no one knows what is going on in the marriages of others. I don't think that our marriage was that much different than many. It just seemed as though we had more difficulties than others. Yet one factor remained—our covenant made before God, family, and friends that we would not quit.

Peace in the Midst of the Storm

It was after a period of almost thirty years that I came to the end of myself, watched as the storm subsided, and asked Jesus to take it all. It was only then that I began to understand that my purpose on this earth was for Jesus to live through me.

> "I have been crucified with Christ. It is no longer I who live, but Christ who lives in me. And the life I now live in the flesh I live by

faith in the Son of God, who loved me and gave Himself for me" (Galatians 2:20 ESV).

I began a strategy of prayer, meditation, and solitude and allowed the thoughts of God to infiltrate my mind. The Bible speaks a lot about renewing your mind. Thoughts are a result of belief. Actions follow thoughts. Slowly, I began to experience a new love for Brenda, others, and myself. Did I mention that determined Brenda found a doctor in California who could repair her female parts and restore her ability and desire for intimacy? Since I'm getting a little too personal, there's no more I need to write about that.

I remember a story I heard as a child about the bear that climbed over the mountain to see what he could see. Climbing a mountain is not easy, but the view on the other side is worth it all. As a result of not giving up and remaining committed, we are in a place that few experience. I can honestly say that Brenda and I have struggled up the mountain, but we have been blessed with a breathtaking view.

I hope that anyone reading this will learn sooner than I did that marriage is a covenant and not a contract. Marriage is two people in communion with God, supporting each other, and providing space for each other to grow.

Gary's Note in The Blest Nest's Guest Book
4/7/2013
Dear Brenda,

Your amazing talents and abilities are in every corner and piece of this place of refuge. During our weekend together, my thoughts have wandered back over almost thirty-six years of marriage and the road we have traveled together to get to this place in our lives.

The road to The Blest Nest is a good representation of our road together—and as He did on the road, God has blessed us at the top of the climb. However, the cabin is not at the top. It is here that we gather strength in this place of quiet and solitude, in the presence of God, to look to the top of the mountain.

As God has blessed us with this cabin, I, like you, pray that many who come here will experience the joy of God's presence and the fulfillment to soar with their own wings to heights that only God will lead them to.

I love you! Gary

On Our Forty-Second Anniversary
5/14/2019

Dear Brenda,

I love your heart, your soul, and your everything. Forty-two years is quite a milestone. I have learned a lot about myself and about you, my amazing wife. The most important thing that I have learned is that all people change, and the person we marry does not stay the same. Marriage becomes a safe place for two people to evolve into who they are. You have provided that safe place for me. I am honored to be your husband and to have provided you that safe place for forty-two years.

As a result of not giving up and remaining committed, we are in a place that few experience. I imagine climbing a mountain where the peak is hidden in the clouds. We have climbed the mountain and have ascended above the clouds. As we stand and look around, we can now look down at what was hidden for a long time and experience the joy and fulfillment that come from seeing what few will ever see and living where few will ever live.

Looking back, I see the many times that God has been our strength and guide. I rest assured that we are here today as a result of our relationship with God and our dependence on Him. On this day, I look back and, with great expectation, look forward to the coming times, that we can continue to grow and experience this level above the clouds.

We are on top of the mountain. There is much to see and experience. Today is the beginning.

I love you! Gary

On Our Forty-Third Christmas Together
12/25/2020

Dear Brenda,

While we are indeed happy and blessed and celebrate the birth of Jesus, I am thankful for the mother you have been and are to our children. All of our children are amazing and followers of Jesus as a result of your life given to them.

God has blessed us with everything we could possibly imagine. We lack for nothing. We live in America, where we are free to be and become, where peace, love, and joy are possible. Most importantly, we walk together with God and have the privilege of knowing and possessing eternal life.

We have so much to be grateful for. I am not lucky. I have been blessed by God. Today, I am thinking of you and how grateful I am for you.

I love you! Gary

On Our Forty-Fourth Christmas Together
12/25/2021
Dear Brenda,

I am more grateful for you than ever. It takes a lot of years to see the puzzle pieces fit. Puzzle pieces that do not fit are just pieces on a table. One piece shows up, then another until the picture is complete. I see clearly now more than ever.

I love you! Gary

New Season: Part Two

2/22/2020

"To fall in love with God is the greatest romance; to seek him the greatest adventure; to find him, the greatest human achievement."

—Attributed to Augustine of Hippo

Gary and I are still married. Thank you, God! *Both* of us agree that, now and in the future, we will talk things through—*together*—when it comes to financial or any other decisions that could affect us both. We have *both* chosen to treat marriage as a partnership, because it is.

Thoughts and beliefs had been distorted, which created a breeding ground for intruders (in the form of both people and things) to encroach upon and invade our lives. Those thoughts and beliefs brought trouble that could have been avoided. It took forty-two years, eight months, and twenty-three days to arrive at this place of new understanding. To better understand and remember important matters in our new season as husband and wife, Gary and I recommitted to unconditionally love one another "from this day forward" on February 6 of this year. When we married on May 14, 1977, we began to build a union based on faith, unconditional love, honesty, trust, and respect. Beginning again with that good, solid foundation will be critical in keeping our strong support system from falling apart due to pressure, stress, and the storms of life.

"The most important of the Lord's work you will ever do will be within the walls of your own homes."[27]

—Harold B. Lee

11/27/2021

During the writing of this book, I reached out to married individuals for tips and comments on what has strengthened their relationships. Help comes when it is needed, and the puzzle pieces eventually find the perfect places and times to fill their prearranged, God-ordained spaces. The manuscript for this book was being turned over to the copyeditor on December 4, 2021. The following contributions came according to God's timing, not mine. My friend Glenda will share words from her heart first, and her longtime best friend, Patsy, will end this chapter.

To preface, Gary and I met Glenda and her husband, Jimmy, on a cruise in October of 2009. They were our crew-appointed breakfast partners each day while on the ship. The subject of marriage came up, and Glenda could tell that I was reaching out for a marital lifeline. She hadn't been feeling well and hadn't wanted to go on the cruise. But she prayed about it and asked God to allow her to meet the people He wanted her to meet. Glenda and I not only met, we also connected at the soul level.

It took me a while to locate Glenda's contact information. She still remembered me after twelve years had passed! I asked if she would write something for my readers about marriage. Without knowing where that writing journey would lead, she started writing from her heart. Courage was gathered and her openness was revealed. Glenda learned that being honest with herself and others could lead to a beautiful story of God's love, protection, provision, faithfulness, mercy, grace, and forgiveness. Her story tells of the life she has shared with Jimmy with God by their side. She thanked me deeply for the unexpected blessing of cleansing that took place within.

Our Story

The foundations were laid years ago for who my husband and I are and why we are where we are now. Having just celebrated our sixtieth anniversary, I've given a lot of thought to how we got here. My father (that term is used lightly in my case) walked out on my mom, my sister, and me when I was in the fourth grade. I can remember that day vividly and the trauma it caused. I had already trusted Christ as my personal Savior and remember my prayer, even at that young age, that my future children would *never* have to experience what I had to go through as a result of the desertion. That remained my prayer as I saw what the desertion did to my mom through the years.

A young man in our community had also been praying for God's guidance for his future. He was the son of my mom's best friend. In fact, his parents paid for my mom's divorce. We knew each other from before I could remember and had never given a thought to ever ending up together. In fact, one guy that I dated actually said he would have to ask my "big brother" if we ever made plans to get married.

The summer that I turned seventeen, our families made a trip to Panama City. My "big brother," as my boyfriend at the time called him, was writing a postcard to a girl he was casually seeing. I teased him about it saying he must *really* like her if he couldn't go a few days without writing to her. He said, "I don't really like her."

"Then why are you writing to her?"

Jimmy replied, "I don't know."

Back and forth we went, and then both of us saw what was right in front of us as we bantered back and forth. I never saw him as a "big brother" again. So, that's the beginning.

We started praying together that day for God to lead us as we sought guidance about what had just happened between us. He was twenty-three years old, and I was an immature seventeen-year-old in high school. *Could this possibly be the direction we should go?* We kept praying for God's guidance as we went forward. Our prayers were quickly answered as we married the next summer.

Jimmy was sent overseas a month after our wedding. That turned into a really long year. Satan worked on me as an eighteen-year-old, and only through God's grace were we able to survive intact. And that was the *easy* year.

Our *real* life started after he came home as we got to know each other again. He was so patient and loving to me as I tried to transition from being a teenager to being a wife. I needed to grow up, without a doubt, and his faith in God and his endurance were what allowed this to happen—eventually. From day one we had morning devotions and prayer together. Jimmy had developed this habit before we were married, and we kept it going as a couple.

Now more background: Even though my mom struggled to raise two girls, she always made sure we had piano lessons. She made sure I practiced every day, and this was always a battle. She never gave in to my temper tantrums, so piano was always in my life. I learned to play over *my* objections, and music became a very important part of my life.

Shortly after our marriage, I became the church pianist for twenty-five-plus years. This required much of my time, but Jimmy was always so supportive while I spent hours practicing and attending services. I was also playing at many other things outside the church (civic events, weddings, and funerals as well as judging talent shows, teaching piano, etc.). All were worthy things but very time-consuming. Through it all, Jimmy was supportive and never complained. He spent nearly all day on Sunday and every Wednesday night watching our two small children while I was at practices. I loved the Lord and had dedicated my life and talent to Him. This was my way of offering service to my Lord. I was never happier than when I was praising God through my playing. For many years, this was my life.

Jimmy was still so faithful in his daily Bible reading and prayer before he left for work in the mornings. I joined him most mornings but began to let other things take priority.

I don't know when or how it happened, but I became proud of my ability to play so well. *Boy, was I good!* Then fear set in over not being perfect when I played. What if I missed a note? Or missed being on time for an entrance? That would be unacceptable! That's when I started having panic attacks when I played. No one was aware of this but me. The joy I always had in playing the piano for God was gone. It was *all* about me! The panic attacks were something I cannot describe. Uncontrollable. And I couldn't share it with anyone. So I kept it to myself and began hating the thought of attending church because of it. I really thought I was losing my mind! So I suffered in silence. Jimmy questioned me many times about what was wrong, but I couldn't admit it to him. I couldn't even admit it to myself.

Meanwhile, Jimmy was always a faithful servant of God, starting his day with Bible reading and prayer. I seldom if ever joined him anymore. He was always the spiritual leader, serving faithfully as protector and provider for our family.

I started having some serious illnesses at about age fifty. I was still playing the piano at many events. The panic attacks were taking a toll on me physically and mentally. I was taking it out on my family, and it was evident that something had to change. So I just quit! Just flat-out quit—right in the middle of preparation for a Christmas musical. The panic attacks were gone, but depression set in. This was a dark, dark two-year period.

Meanwhile, Jimmy was still the faithful, steady husband he had always been. Doing his Bible reading and prayer time every morning. *Alone!* He was praying for me and seeing that I got the help I needed to get through it. He never gave up on me—such a man of God he has always been.

I was angry also. Why had all this happened to me? I had tried to do everything right. I questioned everything: God and my faith. Where was God? Praise the Lord for a great Christian counselor, my mom, my pastor, Jimmy, and a really great friend. I finally began to recover from this terrible place.

I had to face some things about myself that were very difficult. The answer was so simple. I had taken my eyes off the Lord, who gave His life for me, and only saw myself. God had not left me, but I had certainly wandered from Him. This was not a quick healing and may not have been the only reason for my depression, but I am sure it contributed greatly. Only through prayer, fasting, God's Word, quiet devotion time and, yes, meds was I able to finally pull my way up through that dark place.

Meanwhile, Jimmy was still right there loving and supporting as he had always done. Now, after sixty years as I reflect over our life together, I stand amazed. The love of our Lord we now serve together grows sweeter each passing day. Through all the years before, we were at the church building many times during the week. Jimmy was there because of the Lord he served, and I was there because of who I was! But God never gave up on me and neither did Jimmy. My husband is such a gift, and I am beyond thankful for him.

It was only through God's grace and abundant love that we survived all those years. It took way too many years for me to appreciate all that God had so richly granted me. He truly honored my childlike prayer in spite of me. Being a church pianist is not a bad thing. It was what I let it become that was wrong. What a revelation!

Since that time our marriage has been totally different. We have been united like never before in honoring God's place in our lives. Was I happy before? I thought I was. But did I have joy? Far from it. I can't put my finger on any one event that caused me to listen to God's conviction.

Looking back, I realize what I missed through those years. Without both partners allowing God to be LORD OF ALL AND IN ALL, there is no unity. From that time on, there has been true love and appreciation for each other.

I went years never playing the piano and came close to selling it until I realized the piano was not the problem. I was! Now I spend many hours having my own personal church services.

Conclusion: In all the years of our marriage, we have not been unique in the trials of life. We have experienced death of family, disappointment, financial issues, broken trust, betrayal, and more. But God is faithful, and we now look to Him *together* for comfort and strength at those times. Now in our retirement years, as we reflect on all the ups and downs, the downs just fade away.

It has been very difficult for me to put this on paper and admit my failures as a follower of Christ. My friends and family would never have known these things had I not written this. We can fool others, but there is no fooling God. I asked for forgiveness, and He graciously forgave me and allowed me to forgive myself.

My prayer is that this may help someone else to be honest with themselves. We are imperfect, but God is perfect and stands ready to forgive and give peace like you've never known.

12/3/2021

Today, I had the honor and privilege of receiving a letter from Glenda's friend Patsy. Glenda and Patsy met as toddlers and walked through life together as best friends. Glenda volunteered Patsy to write words of marital wisdom for this book based on personal experiences. Patsy took the important matter to heart. With gratitude and awe, I share Patsy's words, written on November 27, 2021.

Three Intertwined

Here I sit, favorite coffee cup in hand, staring out at a beautiful canvas of rich fall colors. Deep reds, brilliant yellows, fading purples, and various shades of green surround my quiet corner on the back porch of the place I call home. As my thoughts drift toward Thanksgiving and my many blessings, I notice the soft chirping sounds of some remaining songbirds, which add to the peace and pleasure found in my world of privacy. How blessed I am to have such a place, where I can come to recall the blessings of the day or even those blessings of a lifetime.

There is great joy to be found in these moments of meeting once again with my past—a past that challenged my husband and me to grow a relationship that was to be centered around three rather than two partners. On this Thanksgiving, we will be giving thanks for our sixty-one years of marriage that survived many tests and trials. Over time, the hard times led to our strong family relationship, centered around love, respect, and forgiveness for each member.

Our marital relationship has been healthy and long-lasting due to us being raised in godly homes. We were both nourished in the safe and secure surroundings of the conservative and moral beliefs of strong, caring parents. Daily examples of these individuals exhibiting their faith, their trust, and their respect for one another provided the foundational aspects of what would one day help us establish a secure home in which to raise a family. This was an excellent visual of a moral home in which love could grow.

Since the word *love* could mean a variety of things when being used, it was important for both of us to clarify and precisely communicate the desired definition of such a powerful, influential word. We believed a correct understanding of each individual's meaning would be crucial for the survival of our relationship. This extra yet important work led to many hours of pre-marital and post-marital discussion.

Talk, talk, and more talk about love was to become a jumping-off point to learning more about our emotions, likes, and dislikes. It seemed that anything and everything led to the topic of love. This was a growing time for each of us and was establishing the beginning of a lifelong trait of our marriage. Up to the present time, talking has been a natural part of finding solutions for the many issues that entered our lives.

After these discussions, we began to recognize that the type of love we desired to rule over our life together could be learned only as we discovered and learned more about God since God *is* love. Growing from this love, we believed we could learn to express to each other traits of greater kindness, patience, gentleness, and joy. As time passed, we saw additional traits such as self-control and peace become a part of our daily routines.

The love we sought for our lives was not to be just a feeling of liking each other. We wanted more, a lifelong unity. To achieve this unity, we chose to ask God to partner with us to add additional strength to our union. After reading Ecclesiastes 4:12 (NASB), which states, "And if one can overpower him who is alone, two can resist him. A cord of three *strands* is not quickly torn apart," we determined this union was to be a partnership of three for life. It was to be a relationship in which we could freely, willingly ask for and receive from God the grace needed for particular situations and needs. Intertwined with each other and with God, we knew we would never be nor feel alone. This was easy for us to think or say we believed, but when tests and trials come, the truth of what we have been so confident about may reveal flaws due to our own weakness of not trusting our partnership with God, our partnership of three.

We did not have to wait long to discover just how strongly our beliefs would be evidenced in our choices during our personal tests and trials. Little had we expected the many and unusual trials and tests that would fill our life together, starting with the first year of marriage and the choices we made. That year would become like a training ground for growing faith and trust in our new partnership. We found our faith did rise in the face of our mounting fears, doubts, and questioning that occurred when our first child, Dawn, was born with spina bifida and other deformities. This was during a time when very little was known medically about how to help her survive. We were granted three years with her before the Lord took her to dwell with Him.

As we drew closer to God, we were blessed with the love and encouragement of wonderful, godly friends. In the following years, no matter where we went, our lives were filled with laughter, singing, games, and fellowship centered around the blessing of godly, dear people. There was always encouragement during the most difficult times because of God's provision of friends to the marriage.

Learning to trust God with all of the daily issues surrounding Dawn and adjusting to all the new responsibilities of this huge test was crucial. However, there was more to come. We had to face the shocking news that Dawn's father (my husband) had been in a mining accident that left his spine fractured, his leg crushed, and him unable to work for a considerable time. Talk about a need for a rush job on building faith! Fears and questions rushed to the forefront of our minds. How would our many needs be met? Where were the resources to fulfill our obligations? How would we keep our spirits up as more tests entered our days?

We turned to prayer and chose to trust our partner, God. We also began to look for God's good, which could be found in each dark situation that made up every circumstance. We determined after a while that our happiness did not depend upon our circumstances. We chose to know we could get through the challenges found in the present as well as the challenges of the future. With this knowledge and reassurance, we chose to find joy in the situations rather than look at the grief and stress found deep within them.

The tests and challenges continued in the years that followed. Each one proved to be a growing experience with lessons from God on faith. There were challenges, including death, sickness, dangers associated with being a policeman (my husband), and returning to college while raising three children. The list continues, involving many degrees of struggle and pain, but our partnership of three endured.

Those early lessons of accepting God's will for our lives and praying fully without bitterness prepared us for the many challenges our future held. Early in our marriage, we agreed never to go to bed angry with each other (not an easy thing to always do). There were times of pouting until the anger had passed, followed by talking and forgiveness. We often distanced ourselves from each other until we calmed down, but we always reached a resolution of peace between us before going to bed.

The ultimate solutions always called for talking and talking, which involved many all-nighters, to understand each other's views on matters. But in our home, harsh disagreements and fights had no place. This decision helped us make the call not to allow alcohol or drugs in our home. We chose to avoid those influences, which could have possibly added disruption to the peace and joy in our minds and our home. We found that our prayers and forgiveness were sources of healing in unrestful, stressful situations.

As our children entered adulthood, our stress took on a different form as we watched them face their own tests and challenges that would grow their faith. But we still applied the early lessons that had always proved invaluable in our marriage. We encouraged them to partner with God, to build on His principles, make wise choices, and seek peace and joy. We taught them that from birth until death, life would always be a learning, growing process for each new generation.

We are now entering a new phase of our life together that will bring with it new physical and mental trials that come with age. It's a fearful time because aging does create new problems in achieving the solutions needed for certain problems. But we know Who is intertwined with us in this portion of our journey. He has permitted us to be wherever we might be, and our reaction to the circumstances will be for His purposes, to bring honor and glory to His name. This knowledge of His being in control of all circumstances promotes peace, love, and joy in our union. We look forward to many more years intertwined with God and experiencing His growing process.

Turning Old into Gold

9/12/2020, 7:37 a.m.

Two supportive words have been planted in my mind; they have begun to grow. The two words are *forgiveness* and *resilience.* It was for my benefit and the benefit of others that I entered this wide, open field of beauty, love, self-respect, growth, and freedom. It helped me become a more forgiving and resilient person.

> "Surely it was for my benefit that I suffered such anguish. In your love you kept me from the pit of destruction; you have put all my sins behind your back."
>
> —Isaiah 38:17

Lyn Worsley is the director and senior clinical psychologist at The Resilience Centre in Epping New South Wales, a suburb of Sydney, Australia. She posted an excellent article on April 15, 2013, titled "Forgiveness and Resilience: How can I forgive when it hurts so much" (https://www.theresiliencecentre.com.au/2013/04/15/forgiveness-and-resilience/). It was perfect for this time in my life when I was wrestling with much to forgive. Being prepared to walk in forgiveness and being "fore-giving" are my ultimate destinations. How do I get from where I am at this moment to where I want to be after these chapters in my life are complete?

In planning ahead, I am reminded of a sign outside a church that shared a pointed message: "God never asks us to understand Him but just to obey Him." Forgiveness is a necessary beginning to living a life of freedom, freed from all that encumbers. Freedom is God's desire for each of us. Obedience requires a humble heart to follow His lead, not ours.

> "Trust in the LORD with all your heart; do not depend on your own understanding. Seek his will in all you do, and he will show you which path to take."
>
> —Proverbs 3:5–6 NLT

The sign outside the same church had another eye-opener posted earlier: "Just love everyone; I'll sort them out later. —God".

Coming to terms with this next truth and putting it into action will aid in creating a joyous life amidst the trials, troubles, and adversities that are part of being human: "For if you forgive other people when they sin against you, your heavenly Father will also forgive you" (Matthew 6:14). It is imperative that we forgive others and ourselves. The heavenly Father always knows what is best for His children. Romans 3:10 can serve as a helpful daily reminder: "As it is written: 'There is no one righteous, not even one.'"

In making the choice to hunker down and feel the trauma and hurt of betrayal, verbal abuse, emotional abuse, emotional manipulation, financial abuse, sexual abuse, identity theft, critical comments, invalidation, belittling, and sarcastic remarks, I needed time. It became necessary for me to visualize and write down each person's name, what they did, said, or didn't do or say, and how each of those parts and pieces made me feel. I wrote a poem on November 7, 2008, titled "Time-Out." The last four lines read:

Anger engulfs me, and I get so mad.
What I feel like doing would be rather bad.
So instead of succumbing and raging about,
I make the best choice and put myself in time-out.

When I woke up this morning with the words *forgiveness* and *resilience* rolling around in my mind, I had to be proactive and do more research. That's when I found Lyn Worsley and The Resilience Centre. But that was not all. Through her, I learned about an amazing man named Everett L. Worthington, Jr., PhD. He is a researcher, professor, teacher, clinical psychologist, author, and advocate who helps individuals forgive others and themselves. His website states his mission is to "help individuals (every heart), couples and families (every home), and even communities and countries (every homeland) forgive."[28]

The following portion of his teachings (*REACH Forgiveness of Others*) can be found on his website (evworthington-forgiveness.com). Dr. Worthington gave me his permission to enter his mission statement and the *REACH Forgiveness of Others* model in my book to help us all understand forgiveness on a deeper level.

REACH Forgiveness of Others

R = Recall the hurt.

To heal, you have to face the fact that you've been hurt. Make up your mind not to be snarky (i.e., nasty and hurtful), not to treat yourself like a victim, and not to treat the other person as a jerk. Make a decision to forgive. Decide that you are not going to pursue payback but you will treat the person as a valuable person.

E = Empathize with your partner.

Empathy is putting yourself in the other person's chair. Pretend that the other person is in an empty chair across from you. Talk to him. Pour your heart out. Then, when you've had your say, sit in his chair. Talk back to the imaginary you in a way that helps you see why the other person might have wronged you. This builds empathy, and even if you can't empathize, you might feel more sympathy, compassion, or love, which helps you heal from hurt. This allows you to give . . .

A = Altruistic gift.

Give forgiveness as an unselfish, altruistic gift. We all can remember when we wronged someone—maybe a parent, teacher, or friend—and the person forgave us. We felt light and free. And we didn't want to disappoint that person by doing wrong again. By forgiving unselfishly, you can give that same gift to someone who hurt you.

C = Commit.

Once you've forgiven, write a note to yourself—something as simple as, "Today, I forgave [person's name] for hurting me." This helps your forgiveness last.

H = Hold onto forgiveness.

We write notes of commitment because we will almost surely be tempted to doubt that we really forgave. We can re-read our notes. We did forgive.[29]

It is for the benefit of humankind to dig, weed, and love well in order to step out of the unforgiveness trap and discover the amazing gift of forgiveness in our present, which will positively affect our future. My dear friend Debbie Holcombe says, "Happy digging!" On Everett Worthington's website are free resources and videos worth reviewing. I encourage you to dig, explore, learn, grow, forgive, and heal—then pay the valuable and needed information forward.

9/23/2020

When I penned the "Toxicity to Tonicity" chapter, I was writing about a long-standing and draining toxic relationship that needed to be addressed. Forgiveness was given, and the issues were eventually resolved (well, as best they could be). Personal boundaries were set, and I wasn't going to allow myself to put up with ill-treatment from that person any longer. Jealousy, insecurities, and feelings of inadequacy were the core borers that emerged during those years of turmoil. Positively identifying the core borers was crucial in getting to the bottom of why I had been targeted. That doesn't make anything about it okay; it just helped me to understand the perpetrator on a deeper level.

Growing a backbone and standing up for myself was a huge accomplishment. When others relentlessly push our boundaries, disregard our personal interests, and only think about themselves, unnecessary trouble will come. Anyone who behaves that way invites trouble upon themselves, and they become an agent who knowingly or unknowingly is depositing eggs that can hatch and bring trouble into the lives of others. Giving pain a name offers us the opportunity to closely examine what lies beneath thoughts, words, and deeds. Doing this does not right wrongs. What it does is help us realize that not one of us is perfect, we all make mistakes, and we are all in need of forgiveness and must forgive others and ourselves. My sister Beverly chimed in with words that ring true: "Anything that perpetually interferes with what is most important in your life you need to get rid of."

Golden insights come when we are being proactive and seeking answers to perplexing problems. On our bumpy marital road, getting rid of anything that perpetually interfered with what is most important in our lives sometimes meant something had to go, and that didn't mean one of us. There were times when selling something became the best solution to get past obstacles that stood in the way of our progress and interconnectedness as a marital team. After each trying impediment (fill in the blank) was out of the way, we were free to move forward and grow into a faithful, respectful, forgiving, and loving marital team.

The hurt and feelings of betrayal I've experienced during several appalling storms were excruciating. I was left writhing in pain and disbelief over the repulsive and careless ways I had been treated. To release myself from the pain of those memories, I had to forgive the offenders, allowing me to live out better chapters in my life's journey. Important lessons were learned during those throes of agony. Now, my proverbial antennae come out quickly when I sense trouble before it has the opportunity to strike.

Keen discernment helps limit a person's exposure to sticky, unfortunate situations and can act as a detour sign to help one bypass a regretful decision. Being prepared for obstacles that can appear from out of nowhere is crucial to responding well instead of reacting in hurtful or unhealthy ways. Preparedness is like having a heads-up as I go through life. There is a term used in golf called "fore." It is similar to something I learned in softball so I wouldn't be caught off guard and hit by an oncoming ball. The warning to *keep your eye on the ball* is a helpful reminder that stuff can and does happen, and the way we respond to a hit is important to the outcome.

9/4/2020

Gary and I continue to learn and practice the complex art of communication. We understand the necessity of asking for forgiveness and forgiving each other quickly instead of keeping offenses and hurts concealed. Hiding those feelings would allow them to feed on our hearts, pierce our souls, and damage our connectedness. Both of us learned the hard way that unhealed wounds of the heart pave the way for relationships to suffer and deteriorate. Couples who keep silent run the risk of their unions eventually falling apart.

I had just written the preceding paragraph when Gary rounded the corner holding a printed-out copy containing words that struck a chord in his heart. He said, "This describes what we were just talking about."

I asked, "What is it?"

"A friend of mine just posted this for anyone to read, and I thought you'd like to read it."

"Reflections on Marriage" was posted by Pam K. today. With her permission, I share beautifully written words from her heart, which are enlightening and fitting for our new season as bride and groom.

This is a vulnerable share. I almost didn't post, but breaking the fairy-tale fantasy of what partnership is has been so freeing for Jason and me.

Reflections on Marriage

Day by day. Year by year.

Am I looking at him? Or a perceived idea of who he is?

When I look at him, do I really see him, or someone from my past? A past hurt or past interaction?

Yes and no to all of it.

Each day breaking through layers of non-truth to unveil the beautiful woman in the mirror, and the respectful and kind man in front of me.

We get to meet each other in the new. A daily choice and ritual. A meeting of equals, friends, companions, lovers, parents, adventurers.

Sometimes one of us needs to surrender first, while one of us breathes deep into courage.

Don't we all want to be seen? Cherished? Celebrated for our wholeness?

We choose to clean out the places within that were closed for renovations. The spaces inside that tell us don't trust, don't share, they won't understand, before we even dare.

It's all a lie. If I remember who I really am, I am enough. So is he.

We don't need each other to be filled.

But it sure is nice to share a soft, gentle touch; a warm cup of coffee; or sit together in the cold night air.

To be held. To be seen. To be adored. To be desired.

These are some of life's greatest pleasures.

When I doubt, and fear speaks loudly—I remember our girls.

I remember how much I wanted to see love in action as a child. I yearned to know it existed. That my parents would fall in love in front of me and I would be witness to that magic.

I remember that longing for myself, for Jason, and for our girls. It's up to us to create magic. To show them what true love looks like, feels like, and acts like.

Everything we need is in us. Trust. Take a deep breath, and jump in. True Love awaits.

Thank you, Pam, for sharing these remarkable insights and for illuminating golden nuggets of truth. It's never too late to create marital magic. It takes two committed, willing, and loving hearts to bring that magic to life. Choosing to live joyfully ever after is a dream worth chasing, fighting for, and achieving every day. The magic is created in our minds, grows in our hearts, and emerges as something beautiful, amazing, and worth savoring.

Some differences and relationships can reach a state of being irreconcilable or irreparable. It is valuable to restore that which is salvageable and to learn from the process of overcoming. Being willing to be taught is a gift we give ourselves. A willingness to teach is birthed from within. Teaching what we learn is a gift that keeps on giving. Mental and visual reminders placed in our paths help us remember how much we've grown, realize how far we've come, and recognize that there's a lot more to learn about life.

Bruce and Toni Hebel's book titled *Forgiving Forward: Unleashing the Forgiveness Revolution*[30] helped me find the key to free myself from the shackles and torment I've experienced in life. Reading through their book for a second time has been like putting forgiveness under a microscope and gaining new insight into what the gospel message is all about. Total forgiveness can only come through the shed blood of Jesus along with His love, grace, and mercy.

To exercise the freedom to forgive, we must ask God to empower us to love other people in a way we can only do through Him. God is love and has gone before us to give us all we need to forgive. Our own humanness is not enough to enable us to totally forgive. Believing that the blood of Jesus paid for the wounds we have suffered—and choosing to forgive by the power of the Spirit—is the only way to get to the other side of forgiving, where true love and peace that passes all understanding awaits.

During my discovery stage of dissecting forgiveness, Bruce and Toni shared a book that was used by God to impact their lives and bring about change in the lives of countless others. God turned the pain and suffering of Bruce, Toni, and their family into a magnificent, life-changing, higher purpose filled with hope, healing, peace, love, and joy. Bruce and Toni became the founders of a worldwide ministry, birthed from their healing place, that is helping change the world one heart at a time. (See forgivingforward.com.)

The book Bruce and Toni shared with their readers was written by Dr. R. T. Kendall. His book helps the reader understand that forgiveness is a choice, sometimes a series of choices. He teaches about the challenge and necessity of taking care of personal business related to forgiving. Birthed as a result of all Dr. Kendall learned during painful life experiences, his book *Total Forgiveness* has the perfect title. Before I even opened the book, the words on the cover spoke volumes: *When Everything in You Wants to Hold a Grudge, Point a Finger, and Remember the Pain—God Wants You to Lay It All Aside.*[31] I knew Dr. Kendall would understand where I've been, where I am, and where I long to be—totally free.

7/29/2020

Absorbing forgiveness and understanding what it truly means to forgive helps me freely give it without prolonged reservations. Through a willingness to explore the complexities and intricacies that make up true and total forgiveness, I now understand how much of one's life an unforgiving spirit undermines and steals. We hurt ourselves the most when unforgiveness becomes an accepted, everyday part of our lives. It is sin, plain and simple. And it grieves the Holy Spirit. Freedom and relief from all that binds is like God untying the knot that kept us in an ineffective state of being. Adding a wrong to a wrong doesn't make either wrong right. It just makes things worse. Doing the right thing by forgiving works wonders. It's about taking personal responsibility for our part and letting God work out the other parts in His way, in His time.

Serving the Lord is not always easy. Forgiving others and ourselves and receiving forgiveness are vital ways to serve the Lord. It's not easy to be joyful and glad and sing when we have been deeply hurt. Yet God always has the perfect cure for that which ails and derails us. I love the way Psalm 100:1–5 is worded in *The Message* version of the Bible.

> On your feet now—applaud GOD! Bring a gift of laughter, sing yourselves into his presence. Know this: GOD is God, and God, GOD. He made us; we didn't make him. We're his people, his well-tended sheep. Enter with the password: "Thank you!" Make yourselves at home, talking praise. Thank him. Worship him. For GOD is sheer beauty, all-generous in love, loyal always and ever.

God knows our pain and knows everything we've been through. He is with us through every step in our life journeys. Our heavenly Father knows what will get our attention to teach us what we need to learn so we can grow, love, care, and share. Trusting God through everything, no matter how bad things might get, is not easy. However, the hands of God are miraculous, and His works are marked with His loving fingerprints. My instructions are to follow the Leader (Jesus). In living and forgiving, it is an excellent decision to follow the example of the One who loves most, knows best, and forgave the sins of the world. Forgive to really live.

Afterword to Turning Old into Gold

8/25/2021

This morning, I received a timely devotional via email from Proverbs 31 Ministries. It became apparent that Tricia Lott Williford posted "Making Space for God to Work" just for me to see on this particular day. I will forever be grateful for Tricia's God-inspired words: "When we show up to do our work, we make space for God to do His."[32] Those words helped corral my heart, holding back words that could escape and cause harm to another person.

I showed up this morning with tears in my eyes to do *my work*. That work was writing a letter to a person who had triggered and exasperated me to the nth degree. Forgiving that person over and over and over had gotten old. I forgave again because I knew I must.

Before I began writing the letter, I prayed. My intent and heart's desire was to speak the truth in love, not from a place of hurt. It was received well by two people who were not the addressee. (They have been confidential sounding boards throughout this process, so I was not spreading gossip.) The letter spoke powerful, life-giving words and inspiration into my sounding boards, especially one. However, it became clear that the words contained in the letter, while true, would have a devastating effect on the intended recipient. As it turned out, the words in the letter were meant for me. They helped me realize that I'm still hurting from parts of my past that are keeping pain alive in my present.

Of deepest concern regarding my offender is the condition of the person's spiritual heart. The way this person treats others makes me wonder if there was a time when they decided to follow Jesus. Galatians 5:22–23 is a good indicator of what is going on in a person's heart: "But the fruit of the Spirit is love, joy, peace, forbearance, kindness, goodness, faithfulness, gentleness and self-control." I've had to check myself many times about what is coming out of my mouth and the attitude of my heart! When unconditional love is not coming out in words, behaviors, and actions, *love* falls on deaf ears. My offender seriously believes they have been—and still are—justified regarding the ill-spirited way they think and speak.

The best way I can help is to pray for healing to enter their heart. Pray that they will see their hurtful ways, make amends on this side of Heaven, ask for forgiveness, and grow to genuinely love God and others the way God loves them. Matthew 19:26 tells us "with men this is impossible; but with God all things are possible" (KJV).

Today's devotional included words from Tricia's new book. She reminded me that "the Holy Spirit offers the most powerful kind of Together Work." Her book, *This Book Is for You: Loving God's Words in Your Actual Life,* was published eight days before her devotional for today was posted. (There's the number eight again, symbolic of new beginnings!) I purchased Tricia's book and discovered that the Holy Spirit placed Tricia's post to point me toward the words I needed to see and the message I needed to receive. What I choose to do after reading the words God laid on her heart will be up to me. In her book, Tricia states that "God can take what we do and do something with it that we could never imagine."[33]

On this beautiful letter-writing Wednesday in August, good energy was being poured into my soul through Colossians 3:13: "Bear with each other and forgive one another if any of you has a grievance against someone. Forgive as the Lord forgave you." Writing the letter to my offender enabled me to have a change of heart. Instead of delivering the letter to the intended recipient, I kept the letter as a valuable treasure. Since I was the real recipient, I chose to squeeze the juice out of this lesson.

Another lesson for the day was found in Romans 12:18: "If possible, so far as it depends on you, live peaceably with all" (ESV). Praying for my offender daily is an effective way to show up to do *my work,* which makes space for God to do His. Trusting that God is working on our behalf behind the scenes helps me remain at peace with however He chooses to turn the old into gold. When we turn our focus from the faults and shortcomings of others, beauty can become visible in our inner and outer worlds. Our perspective on the offending person or situation changes when we seek help from above instead of relying on our own strength to make positive change happen. Hard "heart" news is often necessary to till the ground in preparation for better seeds to be planted, take root, and grow into a bountiful harvest. Jesus reminds me in John 15:5, "I am the vine; you are the branches. If you remain in me and I in you, you will bear much fruit; apart from me you can do nothing."

Picture Excellence, Not Perfection

8/29/2020

Individual works of art and their frames have stories to share if we'll patiently watch and attentively listen to all they show and tell our hearts. One unique work of art and its frame entered my life during the season when forgiving hurts of the past was in the present tense. Multiple parts of my past had not been released, and I was on the hook to let them all go. Forgiving was mandatory in order for me to be released from the sin of an unforgiving heart. It was essential for my well-being to take good care of myself as a whole.

I've successfully restored broken things in the past, and my sister Elaine knew I could repair our friend's broken frame that had suffered a great fall. An excellent metaphor came to me as I was putting the pieces of the frame together for better. On July 27 of this year, I booked a quaint cottage in the mountains so I could complete important chapters on forgiveness. The broken frame came into my life one month later. It became a fine mental and visual aid that illustrated forgiveness to me in an understandable way.

I've heard that forgiveness is a decision, and I agree. However, there is plenty to process regarding forgiveness. Discovering that it's a decision was a shocker that helped me understand forgiveness on a deeper level. Just saying the words "I forgive you" doesn't give the other person enough information and leaves important parts of the message, and associated feelings, dangling and unprocessed. After I was given the broken frame and the individual pieces of art it had surrounded, I carefully placed them in my car. The outermost shattered edges and the parts closest to the center that remained unbroken needed to be protected so further damage could not occur while en route to my Fix-It Shoppe. Two adjoining sides of the frame were precariously hanging on to one another with nothing but a tiny sliver of metal to keep them together.

This labor of love was a joy as I restored the frame back to readiness for a useful and beautiful life. The frame spoke to my heart in its unhealed state, but the frame and art as a whole now radiates forgiveness. It was made stronger, and the lessons the work delivered were well received.

After rebuilding and strengthening the frame, I can better understand the act and artfulness of forgiveness. Throwing a blanket over numerous offenses and uttering the words "I forgive you" leaves important matters on the table, keeps our pain alive, and allows the root of bitterness to breed new offspring. Grudges against others can take on lives of their own. We become the ones entangled in traps we set ourselves by not making the choice to totally forgive. Sometimes, what we don't know can hurt us.

Secondary revelations were easily seen as I worked on restoring the broken frame. A pointed reminder emerged regarding how quickly long-term relationships can come apart at the seams when the last straw is laid, breaking the camel's back. Relationships need trust in order to survive. When trust has been broken and one realizes, through the valuable gifts of time and experience, that a relationship is unhealthy, unbalanced, and unfair, one becomes faced with a decision that is no longer hard to make.

A successful surgeon once told me that before he performs actual surgery on a patient, he practices the procedure on inanimate objects that replicate the real thing. As I was chiseling, gluing, filling in, painting, and sealing the picture frame, I wondered what the frame would look like hanging on a wall in an unhealed state surrounding a beautiful work of art. The centermost part would be intact, but the rest would look like a dangly, jagged mess. What statement would I be making if parts of me were hanging on for dear life, not allowing the light within to shine?

It is not a coincidence that I received the broken, tangible item in need of repair at that specific moment in my life. My identification with the frame made it seem to come alive so I could better understand the act of forgiving, realize the need to be quick to forgive, and choose to adopt a mindset of pre-forgiving others and myself. Forgiving others and myself will be a lifelong dance filled with one choice after another. Deciding "yes" before the need to forgive arises will help train me to be proactive and respond responsibly instead of reacting in unhealthy ways to troubles that are sure to come in life.

The scripture verse in the center of the frame was artfully hand-casted, and it turned into being a constant reminder to me that "as for me and my house, we will serve the LORD" (Joshua 24:15 KJV). It is a miracle that the impact of the fall did not compromise the glass, lettering, mat board, or beautiful deckle-edged, handmade paper. Miracles come in many ways, in many forms. Truths told through a broken frame and the preservation of the art within created a perfect picture of God's masterful creativity and His delicate ways of teaching and touching hearts in need.

My Purrfect Garden

8/31/2020

It was time to weed our new home's planting beds. In one particular area of interest, thorny shrubs were in an unhealthy state of being. Upon closer inspection, I saw that viny weeds with wicked thorns were clinging for their lives among the dead and dying shrubs. Immature trees, almost three feet tall, claimed their space in the ground several inches away. It would be impossible to clear the area without removing the unwanted plants.

Each spent shrub and its roots would make perfect kindling for my upcoming forgiveness/letting-go ceremony at a fire pit in the mountains. Thorn-laden vines would be added to the mix. Gary found the perfect-size box for me to transport the already cut-up-in-my-mind uprooted plants. With the box filled to the brim with "thorns of life" that I wouldn't allow to hurt me anymore, I imagined myself feeding the contents of the coffin to the fire and watching peacefully as accumulated pain transformed miraculously into ashes. Turning pain-producing thorns into ashes is a pleasant dream that God will make come true. He will give me these desires of my heart because it is in His will for my heart to heal and for me to live in freedom.

9/3/2020

Clearing the area of the thorny shrubs and their decaying roots was like breathing in fresh air. No longer an eyesore, the earth's freshly prepared canvas was ripe for the artist's painting. Correcting an erosion problem on the steep slope and choosing deer-tolerant and weather-resistant plants will become an ongoing mission to celebrate life on the hill. Our home's previous owner left a special piece of yard art that will be a lovely pendant for the nearby fence to wear.

Restoring neglected areas of our planting bed leads me to think about how easily neglected areas of our lives can become overgrown with, and strangled by, unwanted plants and weeds. An example of an unwanted plant or weed would be an offensive or hurtful comment that enters a person's heart and becomes a source of continual annoyance or trouble. Thorns in people's sides and weeds in life gardens can threaten to steal life away from kind, generous, thoughtful, trusting, caring, and loving souls, yet it doesn't have to be that way.

The particular cottage for my retreat was chosen because its fire pit is private, and the location would be a perfect match for my needs. Foremost on the list of crucial items to pack for my date with God are my Bible, paper, a pen, two books on forgiveness, Tim Keller's book on marriage, a clear decorative jar with a lid, piñon pinewood, a lighter, a coal bucket, four cut-up shrubs with thorns and their roots, sage, work gloves, candles, and good food. The fire pit is located next to Whispering Creek in the mountains of North Carolina. Praying while listening to the crackling fire, hearing the water gently cascading over rocks, and smelling the sweet aroma of the burning pinewood sounds divine.

Who:	Brenda Eller
What:	Forgiveness/Letting-Go Ceremony and Personal Retreat
When:	October 26–29, 2020
Where:	Little Switzerland, NC
Why:	Leaving behind all that holds me back in life
	"Forget the former things; do not dwell on the past.

> See, I am doing a new thing!
> Now it springs up; do you not perceive it?
> I am making a way in the wilderness and streams in the wasteland."
>
> —Isaiah 43:18–19

How: Please continue reading.

We all need to be healed from something. This is my time to make a decision—on a date that I will be able to remember in the future. Knowing I took care of that business on October 27, 2020, for instance, will keep my mind from rewinding, replaying, and feeling the pain of those memories. Saving the ashes in a clear decorative jar will be important to remind me I no longer see or feel the thorns. Instead, I will see ashes that look soft, safe, and comforting. Before the cooled ashes are placed in the jar, they will go through a sifting process. Discarding all parts and pieces that didn't make it through the sifter will leave behind light and fluffy ashes that feel like baby powder. That will be the part worth saving. (Of course, I will enter the date on the jar.) The present and future deserve this time of healing. I deserve all the time, energy, and resources it will take for me to enter heaven on earth, no matter where I am on this world's map. I'll be on the other side of my forgiveness journey soon.

Corrie ten Boom survived the Holocaust and wrote multiple books that tell of God's enduring love to humankind and true forgiveness that can only come from Him. In *The Hiding Place,* Corrie described her struggle to forgive the former Nazi guard who brutally abused countless people in the concentration camp, including Corrie's dear sister, Betsie. I latched onto the prayers Corrie prayed, asking for God's help when she had harbored vengeful thoughts toward him for all the pain and suffering he had caused.

It was a wake-up moment for Corrie when she realized Jesus died for the guard's sins just as He died for hers. She acted in obedience to the Lord's will and prayed, "Lord Jesus, forgive me and help me to forgive him."[34] Then she prayed, "Jesus, I cannot forgive him. Give me Your forgiveness." And through obedience to the Lord, Corrie forgave the former Nazi guard. Being obedient to the Holy Spirit's prompting worked. It always does. Corrie paid forgiveness forward in the way our heavenly Father wants all His children to do. What an amazing example to follow!

We can know we've sincerely forgiven another from the heart when we become able to pray for those who have hurt us by name and ask God to bless them without expecting anything in return. I'm slowly getting to that place.

Afterword to My Purrfect Garden

10/27/2020, 9:45 a.m.

Preparing for the forgiveness/letting-go ceremony has been time well spent. The ride to the cottage was perfect—no traffic, great weather. The gorgeous Blue Ridge Mountains brought inner smiles around every curve. In the solitude and peaceful surroundings, I have written (and am still writing) letters to people who have been agents of pain in my life, myself included. This ceremony marked with great purpose is something I can do to bring about wonderful change and healing within my soul.

The high today will be seventy degrees, and the sky is bright blue. A salamander greeted me yesterday when I visited the fire pit; it was resting on a rock in Whispering Creek. After writing twenty-six letters that the addressees (thankfully) will never read, I have acquired writer's cramp. However, I am done with the hardest part of the process.

Cleaning out the fire pit was easy with the military shovel my dad gave me several years ago. The thorny contents of the coffin came out in bundles since the horns (I mean *thorns)* locked themselves together in a last-ditch effort to survive. I was grateful for a beautiful day. I donned my purple "It is well with my soul" T-shirt (©Kerusso) and carried piñon firewood, a pile of handwritten letters, and the lighter to the fire pit.

The aroma of burning wood was just as I had imagined. Leaves fell around me as if they were snow. White, fluffy clouds looked like cotton balls against the blue sky. The sound of the rushing water from the creek was mesmerizing.

At 6 p.m., it was over. There were no fireworks, but I knew God was pleased. My part had been to let it all go and turn it over to Him. None of this should have ever been my load to carry. I welcomed joy and peace back into my life.

10/28/2020, 8:00 a.m.

Heavy storms from Hurricane Zeta should be arriving this morning around ten. I needed to gather the ashes from the fire pit to keep them dry. As I carried the coal bucket and shovel down the steep hill to the fire pit, I heard birds greeting me along the path. The powdery white ashes were a welcome sight, and I scooped them up for safekeeping. More birds were heard as I walked up the hill to the safety of the cottage. The only birds I heard this morning were cardinals! To me, cardinals are symbolic of angels. Angels in paradise were letting me know God had heard my earnest prayers yesterday and that all is now well with my soul. Somehow birds just know.

Breaking Ground

9/18/2021

Breaking ground is the point at which solid foundations begin. Sometimes things have to get messy before we can come to the state of being grateful for the good and bad. Reaching a place of full confidence in God's ability to provide enables us to be responsible and do our part, letting Him dig out all that needs to be removed so that blessings can be experienced, embraced, and enjoyed.

An amazing book was discovered in March 2009 when I entered a store to purchase a birthday card and came out with the card and a book. Sue Augustine's book, *When Your Past Is Hurting Your Present: Getting Beyond Fears That Hold You Back,* was timely then and is timely now. Her words, which include the following, breathe life into my present. "The secret to reclaiming inner power lies in taking responsibility for our own conduct, allowing the Holy Spirit to direct our words and deeds, and choosing not to complain and blame others for what we do, think, or say. Reclaiming your inner power has nothing to do with gaining power over someone. In fact, it's quite the opposite. It's more about relinquishing all claims to power in and of yourself, and instead, relying on God's power to transform you, your circumstances, and the other people in your life. Your inner power is not a weapon to be used to destroy, but a tool for building and restoring. It is a way to invite God's power into your life to fulfill your potential and receive your greatest blessings."[35]

Trusting in God's goodness, even when things look torn up on the surface, doesn't mean things are going to remain in their heartbreak-inducing state. God's promises run deeper than we could ever imagine, reach wider than we can comprehend, and are based on the solid rock who will always stand the test of time. Peace can be found in the eye of the storm. When we rest in His truth, keep our thoughts and eyes fixed on Him, and realize that the promises of God will never fail us, we can let go and willingly allow ourselves to be tilled by grace. James 1:2–4 gives us something special to always remember: "Be happy, for when the way is rough, your patience has a chance to grow. So let it grow, and don't try to squirm out of your problems. For when your patience is finally in full bloom, then you will be ready for anything, strong in character, full and complete" (TLB).

THE WILL OF GOD

The will of God will never take you,
Where the grace of God cannot keep you,
Where the arms of God cannot support you,
Where the riches of God cannot supply your needs,
Where the power of God cannot endow you.

The will of God will never take you,
Where the spirit of God cannot work through you,
Where the wisdom of God cannot teach you,
Where the army of God cannot protect you,
Where the hands of God cannot mold you.

The will of God will never take you,
Where the love of God cannot enfold you,
Where the mercies of God cannot sustain you,
Where the peace of God cannot calm your fears,
Where the authority of God cannot overrule for you.

The will of God will never take you,
Where the comfort of God cannot dry your tears,
Where the Word of God cannot feed you,
Where the miracles of God cannot be done for you,
Where the omnipresence of God cannot find you.

Written by: Rebekah Nolt

Delightful Star

Within this new season, a new life is beginning for my friend the tiller. I passed the six-horsepower treasure on to Jeff as a gift since I had no more big plans for her. He needed her help at school and home. For me, the season of doing hard yard work was over. It was February of 2020, and Jeff was serving as the STEAM education facilitator in Tyrone, Georgia. STEAM education combines science, technology, engineering, the arts, and mathematics. The tiller's first project was to assist an Eagle Scout in creating a pollinator garden at a middle school on February 28, 2020.

I named my friend Star because she brought so much joy into my life and continues to be a star in many ways. Life finds fulfillment as we pass our blessings on to others. Knowing that Star will bless others delights my soul.

Star had another new beginning before she could go to school with Jeff and help the students learn in creative and experiential ways. Service and repairs were needed. After receiving a new set of tines, drive belt, valve-cover gasket, getting a tune-up, and having her carburetor cleaned, she was good to go. Knowing she was fit for her particular purpose continues to make me smile. Tilling the ground in preparation for new growth is her specialty. We all need a new start sometimes. Just as Star was destined for more, we too are destined to experience the fullness of the life God created us to live.

When our children were young and I tucked them into bed, I sang them a song I learned in the youth group at church. As I stroked their adorable faces,

I quietly sang "Pass It On,"[36] written and composed by Kurt Kaiser. The lyrics are amazing, and the message will forever ring true. Kurt's life continues to touch hearts as God's message is passed on to the world through song.

The cumulative gardens in my life have made me who I am today. God set me on a mission to write this book for reasons that only He fully knows. Paying His love forward is my heart's desire. As I share my life stories with transparency and authenticity, I pray that these words of hope will inspire others to gather courage, open up, and be honest with themselves and others.

Holding on to false beliefs we've adopted as truth can keep real truths from being exposed. Ask questions and seek guidance from sage ones. Do research on that which puzzles. Learn more about yourself with purpose, courage, honesty, humility, love, and grace. Love others and yourself without conditions. Be kind to others and yourself. Be a delightful star participant in life! Try. Do. Be. Always remember the message revealed in 1 Corinthians 3:7: "It is not the one who plants or the one who waters who is at the center of this process but God, who makes things grow" (MSG).

Fertile Soil

"God has His hands on us all, and He will reinforce our efforts when they honor Him."

—Jeff Eller

2/26/2020

In March of 1980 as I drove to and from work with new life growing inside me, I imagined chatting with our firstborn son or daughter who was close to being birthed. Gary and I had chosen to wait until after the delivery to find out which it would be, to let God's gift to us be a surprise. Three times I received what I inwardly desired—boy, girl, girl. Gary still remembers me smiling and looking down at our seven-pound-ten-ounce precious son saying, "I got myself a fella!"

Even though we were eager to start the process of raising a family, I felt unprepared on multiple levels. When I was a teenager, babysitting had been the only way I learned how to care for children. Somehow I managed to get out of changing diapers. Either the children were older or the parents had already tucked their diaper-clad little one in for the night.

Our growing family was showered with gifts and blessings to celebrate the impending miracle of birth and a precious new life. The nursery was decorated in yellow and green instead of pink or blue. A dear neighbor gave our unborn baby a newborn-size teddy bear. As a new mommy beginning the most important work of my life, I was grateful for that gift! In an effort to stretch funds while transitioning to one income, Gary and I had decided to use cloth diapers instead of "throwing money away" using disposable diapers. In 1980, disposable diapers didn't have elastic around the legs, and I had the mistaken belief that rubber pants over a cloth diaper would keep inevitable messes contained for easier cleanup. Feeling prepared to care for our baby in the best way possible helped reduce my fears of the unknown. After placing the blue teddy bear on the changing table and successfully pinning a cloth diaper together without the diaper pin touching the brave stand-in baby, I felt relieved. Silly, I know, but it helped me feel confident that I could manage that feat.

When our new bundle of joy arrived home, I followed through with our choice to utilize cloth diapers and rubber pants. After a short while of trying to save money that way, I took a detour at the grocery store and started buying disposable diapers. I learned it was easier to dispose of the messes, and we chose to not think about the additional cost. The ease and savings in time were welcomed. Another benefit was that cloth diapers made excellent dusting rags. Live and learn! Josie, a dear friend of mine, was ninety-one years old when she shared this power-packed truth: "Sometimes we have to grow up with our young'uns; I know I did!" Just like Josie, I grew up with our "young'uns," yet I consider each of them to be light years ahead of me. Our children were raised in fertile soil. What we lacked as parents, God gave in abundance. As a family, we have been blessed beyond measure. All the praise and glory go to God!

Our precious grandchildren are so fortunate to have God-fearing parents, and we are blessed to have the joy and privilege of witnessing them being raised in Christ-centered homes. In 2011, Jeff and his wife, Karen, were each nominated as Teacher of the Year at their respective schools. They are star teachers in my book every day of every year. Keep up the great gardening at home, at school, and in your multiple life gardens. Both of you receive giant-size A-pluses, countless shining stars, and smiley faces that smile for miles. I love you and your treasured family dearly!

11/8/2010

We never know how our actions, behaviors, thoughts, and words might inspire, encourage, or challenge another to take positive action in some way. Our thirty-year-old son transferred the following reflections into a handmade Guatemalan journal for me. When Jeff presented this special gift to me after his return to the States, I cried, as he predicted I would, because his compassionate and tender heart had touched mine.

11/5/2010 (ANTIGUA, GUATEMALA)

Mom,

Recording life in writing is a potent possibility that I choose to take on and appreciate the benefit of, especially on this trip. When I was writing an excerpt of an experience yesterday, I shared your process of life realization to those seated around me and was proud to reflect, and then record, careful reflections with the mission team group. Below is an excerpt of the writing, and sharing this with you is an honor.

11/3/10 This morning I cried. I reflected on the need and more so the want. The fabric of my faith was challenged (not with the composition but with the complication). The key to the breakdown was in the image of the eyes, the fish, and the cow.

Everyone has been sharing about the children. The needs of the children are different here than those of the United States. This comparison between Guatemala and "home" is valid because children that reside in the states are influenced by penetrating desires, which infect the rest of their lives.

When the "needs" are reviewed, an itemized list is formed that connects to fundamental yet vital needs of America. The basics—food, water, shelter . . . and one more . . . love. This love is like burning embers, buried in the cooking fire and then uncovered, given a breath of life to burst into sustaining heat as fuel is added. Guatemala has been fuel to my embers towards my love of Jesus and my love for people.

I know these people because of their eyes. Eduardo is twenty-six and married. His wife will have surgery on the fourth and . . . they may lose their first child.

Herman is a good son. He is ten and loves the smaller children and was my "right-hand-man" as the week went on. Melissa cut her hand deeply while slicing oranges. She needed medical care we were not prepared to give, but we did the best with resources. She was brave, she had courage, her eleven-year-old heart was that of a determined panther (even through the tears and pain). Brave . . . brave . . .

Then, the "handshake" of the nameless—so many children. Clap, bump front, bump top, bump bottom, bump elbow—uno, dos, tres, cuatro, cinco. The handshake brought the eyes closer to really get a good look—children of purpose and promise, children of the city, the mountains, the noble families, the children of Samayac . . . deep brown, some squinting, some round, some speaking louder than language can share.

Also, in those moments as the tears welled up, fish came to mind. Yes, fish . . . Samayac is a fish. Christ is the backbone, and all other parts respond to its prompting. The children of Samayac are the ribs that support, protect, flex, grow, and are connected to the backbone. Yes, "all have sinned and fall short of the glory of God" (Romans 3:23), but He still prompts the direction and movement of our life. The scales are prayers: protection, provision, salvation, and awareness of Christ's plan for His glory for future generations. The fins remind me of the sway and bending that attempts to spiral actions and destinations away and off course. Pectoral fins stabilize and allow the fish to pause and take a moment for the "lateral line" to work. A length of nerve cells extending from the head to the tail of the fish (like the Holy Spirit in my life and their life if they choose to accept). At the moment of tears, the fishes have surfaced. The polluted water came to mind!

The children drink the polluted water filled with visual waste as well as the invisible, the deadly microorganisms. Children are infected by the past that defines the present. Physical ailments disguise themselves with costumes of deceit and illusions of an empty hope in a lower case god—the god of a face, a church, a statue, a grave, a relative, but not the God of life—abundant life . . . full of life . . . a life of hope . . .

So predominates the cow. The cow has much to give, but as a consumer and herbivore of substantial size, it cannot assume the potential God set in motion upon creation. The obvious meat can be cut into valuable and less-preferred pieces. The "butcher" knows the cow: knows where, how, when, and how many times a cut can be effective and produce one of the four basic necessities—food. God's love, as a creator and jealous pursuer of recognition of His accomplishments, has graced humanity with a creative streak. Samayac is a community of promise as the unsuspecting cow goes to the butcher and artists extract from the cow with a production of purses, hats, bags, blankets, hammocks, clothing, and food items.

God knows who figuratively holds the "purse" to provide the furthering of God's kingdom. He knows the products of art that show promise and commitment. So the complicated part of my journey is in the depth of a child's eye, the division of the fish, and the creative possibilities of the cow.

The leaving and going back will instigate expectations of home from a new context. The Eduardos, Hermans, and Melissas are the people I knew. They and the children with no names are people I will love. Overall, what happens here should be synonymous with my daily intake of "fish" and "cows" as I digest plans and perspectives that God graces my heart to have the opportunity to imbed in my heart and mind. This is what I want . . . things are actually a bit more simple now! Thank you for having a part in this! Love, Jeff

Perfect Peace

Without knowing what I was doing or where this God-appointed assignment would take me, I started writing this book, following His undeniable directive. Through my wilderness and writing journey, I gained perspectives that would have escaped my notice if I hadn't been forced to both feel them on the ground level and view them from above.

As a result of making countless mistakes, I grew to have a compassionate spirit and forgiving attitude toward others. Any judgments I had harbored in the past flew out the window when I was forced to look in the self-assessment mirror that showed more than I wanted to see and told more than I wanted to hear.

Documenting every detail of my life was not part of this writing journey. Many things were better left unsaid. But pulling every silver strand out of every dark cloud was helpful because it gave me a higher, deeper, and wider perspective of what the word *peace* really means. Trying to avoid conflict, waiting on others to change and get better so I can be relieved of grief, and grasping for anything to trick myself into not feeling overwhelming emotions is not pursuing real peace. Real peace is the peace we receive when we allow God to live in our hearts, minds, and every part of our souls and inner lives—all the time, no matter what.

After documenting important parts of my life, I can look back and "read" about why I spent thirteen-hour days in the yard doing backbreaking work. In putting broken parts back together again in the yard, I was also working on putting shattered pieces of my life back together the best way I could. I became a stronger person as a result of everything I went through and learned. God was speaking to me as I worked on anything that brought peace within. The only problem was this: temporary peace is not eternal peace. It doesn't last; it cannot survive in the long term. Temporary peace is only determined by outward things.

In 2006, when I created the peace plaques, the word *peace* was wood-burned above the design. Below the design, I woodburned the Hebrew writing for *shalom*. Its placement under the design signified how the idea supported the meaning of the work. In the center of the design, I embedded a mustard seed to remind me of the words Jesus said to His disciples in Matthew 17:20: "Truly I tell you, if you have faith as small as a mustard seed, you can say to this mountain, 'Move from here to there,' and it will move. Nothing will be impossible for you."

During those dark days, my faith was growing. It grew deeper and stronger through the years. None of us could possibly know what's around the next corner or at what moment things could change for better or worse. Through the decades of pain I've experienced, God stayed by my side in one way or another, whether I realized He was there or not. I continue to hold this promise near and dear to my heart: "The LORD is a refuge for the oppressed, a stronghold in times of trouble. Those who know your name trust in you, for you, LORD, have never forsaken those who seek you" (Psalm 9:9–10).

I recently found a scribbled note I wrote on May 24, 2017. The words described a season in my life when I had to walk through the fire in order to experience peace on the other side of torment. It reads: "When we voluntarily raise our hand and 'sign up' to help others, we must learn to accept unfortunate happenings because they are there to teach us lessons we may have never learned any other way. Going through the fire does not mean we will not get burned—it means we will have to become heated enough to become pliable, workable, and changeable."

The term "shalom peace" has recently been popping up around me for review and is helping me develop further understanding. When this book began, the following subtitle was foremost on my mind: *Personal Journey to Wholeness and Peace.* Obviously, the subtitle changed, yet the dream of enjoying wholeness and peace within my heart, mind, spirit, and emotions was my ultimate destination. During the emotionally painful times, I longed for tranquility in my spirit, serenity in my mind, and a peaceful atmosphere around me. What I didn't realize at the time is that shalom peace is inner peace and rest in the midst of chaos, conflict, or war. Shalom peace is God's PEACE—God's Presence Experienced, Acknowledging Completeness Embodied. It is having inner peace no matter what events and complications are whirling around me in the world that is upsetting, troubling, and causing pain. Life-giving words of Jesus in John 16:33 bring comfort and reassurance. "I have told you these things, so that in me you may have peace. In this world you will have trouble. But take heart! I have overcome the world." The words of Jesus tie a special and beautiful bow around the present He offers each of us. "I am leaving you with a gift—peace of mind and heart. And the peace I give is a gift the world cannot give. So don't be troubled or afraid" (John 14:27 NLT).

Whether life is going well or life throws punches, shalom peace is a gift presented to us every moment of every day. All we have to do is, by faith and trust in Him, receive God's amazing gift of love—His only begotten Son and His ever-present shalom peace. According to Strong's Concordance (7965), *shalom* means "completeness, soundness, welfare, peace."[37]

Tim Mauricio wrote a devotional that was posted on Calvary Chapel of Santee's website titled "The Irony of Shalom." Tim shared, "For us to look to the true meaning of *shalom,* we must accept that true peace comes from God as a result of our position in Christ Jesus. The peace that transcends all understanding is one based upon an unshakeable foundation of truth, knowing our adoption from God the Father is once for all eternally secure. That our future inheritance in the kingdom has been set aside and awaits our taking possession. That regardless of our circumstances in this present life, we can have and enjoy true peace."[38]

In a timely and inspiring post on the Proverbs 31 Ministries website, Kia Stephens wrote enlightening words. Her post titled "When Pain Prompts Us To Cry Out to God" was published on November 16, 2021, a day when I (once again) believed I was finished writing this book. Kia explains, "God may use our pain to demonstrate His power to humanity. He may use our pain to grow us spiritually. He may use our pain to correct our behavior. . . . We cry out to God in acknowledgment that He is God and we are not. In doing so, we look to Him as controller of the outcome. We pray in faith, knowing that God is more than capable of answering our prayers, but we also accept the reality that He may not answer in the way we want. In doing so, God offers us a peace that persists in spite of the pain we endure. No matter what our pain is, God invites us to cry out to Him."[39]

I've cried out to God countless times, and He has always come through for me in the most creative and miraculous ways. This book was a sincere labor of love. Many people would have abandoned this project and believed it to be too overwhelming, sensitive, time-consuming, expensive, or demanding. But the cost of *not* doing something that God called me to do would have been detrimental to my well-being. I am eternally grateful that God gave me His beautiful and freeing gift called shalom peace.

Planting reminders with words can help me follow my own advice through actions. When troubles come (and they will), I will cry out to God, lay my burdens down at the foot of the cross, breathe deeply, and write this verse one hundred times: "Thou wilt keep him in perfect peace, whose mind is stayed on thee: because he trusteth in thee" (Isaiah 26:3 KJV).

Postscript: Love Much

It is always a joy and privilege to hang out with each of our grandchildren. Abigail is Jeff and Karen's youngest child, and we were having a Grandmom-E/Abigail week when she was four years old. Major spiritual awakenings occurred on the last day of our week together. Truths I needed to know were seen through the eyes of a child and passed on to me. It happened as we were being helpers, making the workload lighter for her mommy and daddy.

As she stood in the kitchen doorway, Abigail looked up at me with wonder and asked, "Grandmom-E, am I an angel?" (She had heard a dear friend call me an angel on the phone earlier in the week.)

I said, "Yes, Abigail, you *are* an angel!"

Her face lit up as she said, "You can have one big wing and one small wing, and I can have one big wing and one small wing. We can be angels together!"

Within minutes, we were tackling our first mission of the day as an angelic team. I had discovered that one side of the kitchen sink was clogged, and Abigail witnessed my determination not to give up plunging until the water moved freely down the drain. The other side of the sink had issues too. "Okay, angel, are you ready? I need your help! Can you climb up in the chair and push on that strainer while I plunge out the other drain?" I asked. She was thrilled to be able to help in a huge way. It wasn't long until both drains were in working order once again.

As I washed the dishes, Abigail played with the bubbles. In the midst of her play, she presented a sensitive question that made me want to disappear momentarily. It was something she had wondered about that seemed to bother her. Even though I cannot remember the exact question, I remember gathering up enough courage to give an answer openly and truthfully without giving unnecessary details. After I had coughed up the answer and gently shared it with confidence, she seemed content with her new knowledge, and I felt relieved. However, it made me wonder what questions she would ask me when she became a teenager! I'm learning, and that experience proved to be excellent training and was digestible food for thought.

Life-application principles can be taught using sinks, drains, clogs, water, strainers, plungers, and helping hands during quality time spent together. In pondering the parallels presented between everyday life experiences and our inner selves, I learned that wisdom can become ingrained when we are involved in the process of gaining understanding. A decision to cease striving can help us enjoy every precious moment with those we love, even while performing mundane tasks. Being present and aware during gifted moments can bring about future blessings. Keeping a positive outlook on situations when life goes wrong can help us "plunge" through the backups in life to help things flow freely once again. Improving ourselves as a whole will create a happy life because happiness can only come from within.

After our dishwashing session, towel-folding teaching time, and running errands, we ate lunch at a fast-food restaurant. In the quietness of the almost empty party room, Abigail looked across the table at me and said, "Grandmom-E, I want to be like you because I like you." My heart melted instantly! However, it didn't take me long to realize this: I had been set apart to be a huge role model in the lives of Abigail and my other grandchildren. Abigail was going to keep me on my toes; she would keep me grounded!

Abigail reminds me of myself as a child. We are deeply connected at the soul level. The influence and responsibility that adults have in nurturing, training, teaching, and coaching the next generation is enormous. Likewise, the influence that children have on adults who choose to learn from the young is monumental. I take my role as Grandmom-E seriously and have the same mindset with these young ones as I did with our three children; I give each of them my personal best.

In this book's infancy, I was given a twenty-one-inch statue of a barefoot little girl. Since the head had been reattached, I knew the statue would represent me well. I often say, "I would lose my head if it wasn't attached." After the lunch date, Abigail and I went to my home for the afternoon. The statue caught her eye, and she became fascinated with the details the artist had created. It was the little girl's eyes that absorbed Abigail's attention the most. She reached for the little girl's head and touched one of her eyes as if to say, "Here, let me help you. What's wrong?" Then she turned to me and said, "Grandmom-E, there's something in her eye. It looks like dirt."

I got down on the floor to see what she saw from her vantage point. I couldn't tell if the eyes had been intentionally left out or if they had fallen out. It made such an impression on me that I decided to make the girl two eyes so she could see. Abigail said, "They need to be white to match the girl."

A parallel lesson about life is this: even if we can physically see, all of us are spiritually blind until we realize the needy states of our own souls. When the dirt is cleared away, we can learn to walk by faith instead of sight. The white color of the eyes represents that which is pure, untainted, unblemished, and stain-free. One doesn't know what one doesn't know until one can recognize what's been missing in their life, and who is needed to fill that void.

Remarkable things can happen when we dig up and let go of something in our lives that is no longer useful or beneficial. Making good changes in our lives will produce excellent rewards. These changes are good investments in our lives and will benefit others in outstanding ways. As we come out of hiding and choose to be gut-honest with ourselves, we can come before God naked yet unashamed. He knows all that hides under our birthday suits. We won't be showing Him anything He hasn't seen or telling Him anything He doesn't already know.

9/25/2021

A close examination of the way my gardens grew helped satisfy my curiosity because I was personally involved in the earlier process of living out these chapters of my life. Choosing to be a willing student gave me the opportunity to more fully understand many of the things that have occurred during my life thus far. Some things are not for me to know, and that's okay. Knowing that God knows all things lets me know He's got this and I don't need to figure everything out or know how things will end.

I thank God I was gifted the time and grace to enter a closer, deeper, and more intimate relationship with my Savior, Redeemer, and Best Friend. As I lean on His understanding instead of my own and take responsibility for my daily thoughts, beliefs, and actions, I will be leaving this world a better place than how it was when I arrived. An ancient proverb reminds me that "all the flowers of tomorrow are in the seeds of today." After putting life puzzles together for better, eight fitting words from Jeff make me smile in agreement: "Things are actually a bit more simple now!"

Indispensable Things

10/26/2015, 8:33 p.m.
Memories come alive between these lines, which help me remember how far I've come, how much I've grown, and how much I need my Savior and Best Friend's help on a daily basis.

Pray first, not last. Take good care of myself. Always remember to never forget: God is I AM; I am not. Do things that help me create a healthy life and happiness. Protect myself mentally, emotionally, physically, and spiritually. Keep a watchful eye on the doorway to my heart. Learn to recognize intruders. Don't let the thieves enter. Call out the name of Jesus if I find them there, then watch them run away. Keep my mind free of clutter and litter. Remove anything that is not useful or healthy in my life.

Embrace and celebrate where I am on my life's path. Don't compare myself with others in any way. Laugh with myself when I don't measure up to my ideals. Tweak my thinking by changing the way I look at things. Don't beat myself up when I realize I followed after folly. Love myself well. Forgive myself. Stop taking life so seriously. Don't go with the flow unless God approves of where the flow is going. Downhill is a downer. Going against the flow may be the way I ought to go. Seek God's help and direction through prayer. Rename and reclaim my life. Create a list of priorities. Set priorities that are in my best interest without allowing myself to feel guilty. These priorities are needed as constant reminders and comforting companions.

Stand up for myself. Be honest with my thoughts and feelings. Express them in honorable ways. Process them as they come. God gave me tears; it is good to cry. When I let thoughts and feelings out, they will not be able to gnaw and grow within. Vent to ones who will give beneficial feedback. Be willing to accept constructive criticism. Being defensive, maintaining a victim's stance, or continuing to deny truth is harmful to every part of my being. Don't compromise sound values and valid principles. Let God be my strength. Weaknesses, vulnerabilities, insecurities, mistakes, short-comings, faults, and failures create a well-balanced fertilizer. God will use these to make a perfect batch of compost to produce profound growth and a bountiful harvest.

Keep my eyes fixed on Christ (looking up), not on things of earth (look-ing straight ahead). Rest in peace while I am alive. Stop worrying about what others think of me. Control my tongue before it controls me. Graciously accept the manna I receive each day. Grumbling and complaining are not allowed. Anything I want—or think I need—may not be what's best. God will take care of my needs according to His plan, not mine.

Love God with my entire being. Fall more deeply in love with Christ. Place my complete trust in Jesus daily. Let the Holy Spirit be my Helper, Teacher, Counselor, Healer, Comforter, Peace, and Guide. Believe in God's Word and in all His ways, truths, and promises. Together, in complete-ness, they will rout out doubt. Be obedient to God. Share God's love with others through unexpected acts of kindness. People are more important than money and things. Love others and myself unconditionally. Consider the other person's interest above my own. Love others enough to let them go if necessary. Release them into God's care. Continue to pray for their well-being. Be kind. Forgive others. Give others the freedom to learn about themselves in their time and seasons and through their own individual processes of development. Let others live their lives as they choose because I cannot change or fix them even if I try. Love them anyway, and pray for them. Listen attentively to others. Offer suggestions instead of giving advice. Use discernment; sometimes all a person needs is a compassionate and nonjudgmental listening ear. A hug may be the perfect unspoken word another needs. Follow the genuine hug with a heartfelt smile. Judging others is a no-no. Trade that time and energy judging myself. Change those things that create woe. Judging is one of those woes that need to go. Respect others. Don't place unrealistic expectations on them. Don't dump my truckful of burdens on others. Don't expect others to bear my burdens, especially those I brought upon myself through personal decisions. Take responsibility for personal decisions. Keep a healthy distance between myself and anyone or anything that steals energy or produces chaos. Genuinely help with a cheerful heart when my helpfulness will be well received and appreciated. I must rein in my overeagerness to jump in and help others. Remember, every person does not want my help. Sometimes our selfish need to prevent others from suffering can actually bring them harm. People rarely choose to change when someone is giving them a false sense of comfort or security. Give generously but with limits to keep personal boundaries in place. Protect myself from being used by others. Being a helper is not the same as being an enabler. There's a difference between enabling others and giving others the opportunity and freedom to become able.

Be a helpful first responder by remaining calm. Respond with behaviors that act as a balm instead of adding to the makings of a proverbial bomb. It will help disarm potential conflicts (aka time bombs). Learn creative and wholesome ways to respond to negative external and internal pressures. Be true to myself and let go of unrealistic expectations. I will have off days when I'm not my usual self. That's okay. I will enjoy a personal pity party but not let that party last for days. A goal of being excellent as opposed to perfect gives me the freedom to enjoy the process of becoming. Accept failure as an important part of that process.

Through Christ, I am valued, loved, validated, and accepted just the way I am. I measure up in God's eyes through His standard of measurement. I am precious in His sight. The attitudes of my heart determine how high I can fly and how far I will go. The Down-to-Earth Wise Owl reminds me again: *Whoooever takes the higher road brings to the table lighter loads!*

Go and be . . .
Grow and become . . .
Sow well and fully live.

"It is for us to make the effort. The result is always in God's hands."
—Kathy Morris, Stroke of Faith

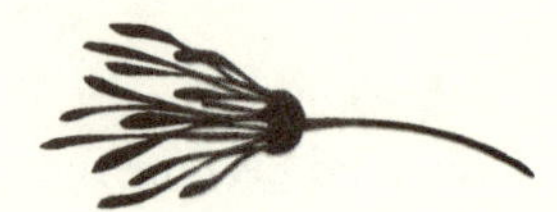

HOW DID MY GARDENS GROW?

I let you see the parts of me
That many hide with lock and key.
My heart was racing when I knew
I had to share or bake and stew.
The great part is I did my best;
God gave me A+ on this test.
To follow through when things got tough
Was hard, yet God's hand smoothed and buffed.
Denying anything that's true
Will rob the very best of you.
When I was called, I said, "I'm in!"
That's when I felt God's great big grin.
No other peace and rest I've known
Compares to how much I have grown.
It's up to you now, my dear friends.
Don't give up 'cause it's not the end.
"How did your gardens grow?" I ask.
The challenge is a worthwhile task.
It's a new day; begin again.
I'll be your most supportive fan.
God gives back more than evil stole.
He forgave, cleansed, and made me whole.

Brenda Eller
10/8/2015, 8:33 a.m.

"For you will go out with joy and be led forth with peace."
—Isaiah 55:12 NASB 1995

Acknowledgments

"How's the book coming?" is a question I was asked countless times by caring individuals. Thirteen years and six months is a long time to stick with such a challenging project. Prayers, encouragement, and support kept me moving toward the finish line, which was this book's publication.

First and foremost, I acknowledge and give thanks to God for making all this possible. Without His help, this book would not exist. And neither would I!

My dear husband, Gary, deserves a gold medal for enduring the marathon with me. He has been a key participant, inspirer, and encourager. Gary cheered me on and supported me in a variety of ways: knocking on the writing-room door and surprising me with delicious cups of coffee prepared just the way I like, bringing home dinner from our favorite restaurants, and giving me space and time to bring this book to fruition. He also gave unbiased feedback on chapters in their developmental stages, which has saved the readers of this book from being bored and saved me from being embarrassed by poor writing. Gary, you saw my writing as an important investment. I will forever value and hold dear the help you gave me in this worthwhile endeavor. I remember the countless times I needed help with how to make the computer do what I needed it to do. Without fail, you stopped what you were doing and came to my rescue. Thank you for being a compassionate and patient teacher. I couldn't have put this book together without you.

I also wish to thank our son, Jeff, who has instilled in me feelings of wonderment. Ever since he was a baby, he has enabled me to view the world of nature through the eyes of a child. I felt the amazement he did as I watched him feel grass for the first time, reach out to touch leaves dancing in the wind, and react with astonishment to a crawling bug. Thank you, Jeff, for all the ways you bring wonder into this world and beauty into my life. I appreciate all the contributions you made to this book and the blessed friendship we share.

Our daughter Erin wears motherhood well. I vividly remember welcoming her into our lives at 3:08 a.m. in January, thirty-nine years ago. Her contributions to this book are heartwarming, thought-provoking, life-changing, and inspiring. Thank you, Erin, for being such an amazing "therapist" and lifelong friend to me. You bring joy, laughter, wisdom, hope, and love to this world and to me. Thank you for all the times you stopped what you were doing to read important chapters and give valuable feedback.

Our daughter Kristyn was married on March 19, 2022, to a perfect gentleman, Ray! This well-known proverb is true: "Good things come to those who wait." Thank you, Kristyn, for the countless lessons you've taught me through the years and for the beautiful gifts of love we've shared that continue to enrich our lives. I appreciate our friendship and enjoy the thrill of watching your gardens grow by leaps and bounds! The constructive feedback you offered on sloppy "early versions" of this manuscript was invaluable and helped keep the dream of publication alive.

To our grandchildren, Noah, Emily, Abigail, and Eli: I fondly remember the time the dump truck dumped topsoil at the end of our driveway. Playing on "the mountain" with each of you kept the kid in me alive! Thank you for bringing into my life a kind of joy and love I never knew was possible. I appreciate the special contributions you brought to this book. Maybe one day Zeke will get to experience playing in the mud with us, and we can all get our feet muddy together. Good dreams are worth dreaming!

To my mom and dad, Peggy and Joe: Thank you for bringing me into this world and helping my gardens in life grow. You sowed seeds of goodness and nourished me with love. Thank you for the many contributions you made to this book. Your support and encouragement are appreciated more than I can express.

My sister Beverly played an important role in bringing this book to life. During countless cherished moments from childhood through adulthood, she was there. I loved playing in the bubbles with her while we washed the dishes when she was ten and I was eight. I still remember singing folk songs with her, which made our work fun. Thank you, Bev, for supporting me, believing in me, and encouraging me to keep going when I had to face tough spots in my story. The contributions you've made in my life are invaluable, and I treasure our deep and special friendship.

My younger sister Elaine also played an important role in bringing this book to life. Through our bond of friendship, a stronger connection was created when both of us entered our new roles as moms. This common thread brought us even closer as more children arrived and our "talks" grew deeper. She became a trusted confidante. Sharing "life" together has been a blessing and allowed us to understand each other on a deeper level. Thank you, Elaine, for being one of my closest friends. Your emotional support and encouragement through the years helped keep me sane while I wrestled with pain. I don't know how I could have made it through the struggles of adulthood without you.

I never realized the depth of the title "editor" until I hired my own. Mary Beth Bishop gently plowed through my manuscript, moved words around, and added words in red that made the black type seem sparse. It was then that I knew I had made the best choice in hiring a true professional. (I feel the need to add her name as a coauthor of this book.) Mary Beth, I acknowledge and appreciate your hard work and diligent efforts to follow through with what you said you would do: polish the manuscript and make it shine. Thank you from the depths of my being. You are truly a star in my book!

This book would not be complete without a cover design that captured the essence of the text. Roy Appalsamy at AMDesign Inc. in Canada did an outstanding job highlighting the most important message of the book: hope. Thank you, Roy, for validating my concerns and making my cover-design dreams come true. Your beautiful work makes me smile!

I am honored to be blessed with a beautiful friend named Shirley Meek Williams. Her foreword at the beginning of this book illustrates the fact we have traveled many miles together and walked on similar paths. Thank you, Shirley, for your close friendship. Your heartfelt words made me remember how much you were there for me, and I cannot thank you enough for that treasured gift. Thank you for your huge contribution to this book and to my life.

I run the risk of leaving someone out if I attempt to acknowledge and thank every single person who contributed to the creation of this book. Therefore,

I will bring you all into a huddle for a huge group hug to show my sincere appreciation. You will know who you are. I will always remember you and the amazing way each of you made me feel. Just as it takes a village to raise a child, it takes a village to bring a book into the world.

Thank you all for helping me bring this labor of love to life!

Endnotes

1 Anthony Sinclair, "Entrepreneurial Spirit," *Powerlines* (GA: Coweta-Fayette EMC, May 2012).

2 Taken from *Keep It Shut: What to Say, How to Say It, and When to Say Nothing at All* by Karen Ehman Copyright © 2015 by Karen Ehman. Used by permission of Zondervan. www.zondervan.com.

3 Barry De Vorzon and Perry Botkin Jr., "Nadia's Theme" (The Young And The Restless), (A&M Records, 1976).

4 Timothy Keller with Kathy Keller, *The Meaning of Marriage: Facing the Complexities of Commitment with the Wisdom of God* (New York: Dutton, Penguin Group USA, 2011).

5 "Benjamin Franklin," AZQuotes.com, Wind and Fly LTD, 2022, accessed April 04, 2022, https://www.azquotes.com/quote/489515.

6 John Keats, *Endymion: A Poetic Romance,* bk. I, line 1.

7 John Wooden with Steve Jamison, *My Personal Best: Life Lessons from an All-American Journey* (McGraw Hill, 2004), 18.

8 Sam Horn, *Tongue Fu!®: How to Deflect, Disarm, and Diffuse Any Verbal Conflict* (New York: St. Martin's Press, 1996), Copyright © 1996 by Sam Horn.

9 Taken from *When You Don't Like Your Story: What If Your Worst Chapters Could Become Your Greatest Victories?* by Sharon Jaynes Copyright © 2021 by Sharon Jaynes. Used by permission of Thomas Nelson. www.thomasnelson.com.

10 Sue Augustine, "Chocolate, Candlelight and Clutter," *Beyond Ordinary Living,* www.sueaugustine.com/articles/chocolate.html.

11 Norman Vincent Peale, *What to Do When Things Upset You* (Carmel, NY: Guideposts Associates, 1974).

12 Taken from *GOD'S WORDS of LIFE From the NIV Women's Devotional Bible* by The Zondervan Corporation Copyright © 1997 by Marjorie Holmes. Used by permission of Zondervan. www.zondervan.com.

13 J. Phillip Landgrave, *Purpose: A Contemporary Musical for Youth*, 2nd printing ed. (Nashville: Broadman Press, 1968).

14 Barbara Rainey and Susan Yates, *Barbara & Susan's Guide to the Empty Nest: Discovering New Purpose, Passion & Your Next Great Adventure* (FamilyLife Publishing, 2008). Revised and updated in 2017 (Bloomington, MN: Bethany House Publishers). Text refers to the 2008 edition.

15 Sydna Massé, *Her Choice to Heal: Finding Spiritual and Emotional Peace After Abortion* (David C. Cook, 2009). First edition published by Charles Victor Publishing in 1998.

16 Colonel Clayton E. Wheat ed., *The Democratic Tradition in America* (Cambridge, England: Ginn and Company, 1943).

17 "Jill Smith Entrekin," Amazon.com, accessed June 26, 2022, https://www.amazon.com/Bucks-Junction-Jill-Smith-Entrekin/dp/0615813267. The subject of the interview is Entrekin's novel titled *Buck's Junction* (Peachtree City, GA: Room 272 Press, 2013).

18 "How to Maintain Your Sanity When You Are Blindsided," Oasis for My Soul: Inspirational Writings for Thirsty Spirits, Tracey L. Moore, Jan. 2, 2020, accessed June 11, 2022, https://traceylmoore.wordpress.com/2020/01/02/how-to-maintain-your-sanity-when-you-are-blindsided/.

19 Paul L. Overstreet and Donald Alan Schlitz (Scarlet Moon Music Inc., Schlitz Don Music, Screen Gems-EMI Music Inc., Universal Music Corporation, 1988).

20 Hannah Flagg Gould, *Poems: Volume I*, "The Crocus's Soliloquy," (Boston: Hilliard, Gray, and Company, 1836), 163.

21 Jaynes, *When You Don't Like Your Story*, 25.

22 "When We Feel Beyond Help" by Corrie Gerbatz, Proverbs 31 Ministries, March 9, 2021, https://proverbs31.org/read/devotions/full-post/2021/03/09/when-we-feel-beyond-help.

23 Shirlee Abbott, commenting on "When We Feel Beyond Help" by Corrie Gerbatz, Proverbs 31 Ministries, March 9, 2021, https://proverbs31.org/read/devotions/full-post/2021/03/09/when-we-feel-beyond-help.

24 "Preserving history: the legacy of Dr. Leila Denmark," 11 Alive, WXIA-TV, May 31, 2019, https://www.11alive.com/article/news/local/mynews/cumming/preserving-history-the-legacy-of-dr-leila-denmark/85-3af110d0-10aa-4c6f-aeee-7ca982fcb32f.

25 Kelly Whitmire, "Legacy of Dr. Denmark lives on through new school," *Forsyth County News* (updated July 30, 2018). https://www.forsythnews.com/local/education/legacy-dr-denmark-lives-through-new-school/.

26 Leila Daughtry-Denmark, M.D., *Every Child Should Have A Chance*, 2nd ed. (Atlanta: Walsworth/W. H. Wolfe Associates, 1971).

ENDNOTES

27 Harold B. Lee, *The Teachings of Harold B. Lee* (Deseret Book Company, 1996), 280. © Harold B. Lee. Used by Permission of Deseret Book Company.

28 "About Everett," Everett Worthington, accessed August 31, 2021, http://www.evworthington-forgiveness.com/about.

29 "REACH Forgiveness of Others," Everett Worthington, accessed August 31, 2021, http://www.evworthington-forgiveness.com/reach-forgiveness-of-others.

30 Dr. Bruce Hebel and Toni Hebel, *Forgiving Forward: Unleashing the Forgiveness Revolution* (Fayetteville, GA: ReGenerating Life Press, 2011).

31 R. T. Kendall, *Total Forgiveness: When Everything in You Wants to Hold a Grudge, Point a Finger, and Remember the Pain—God Wants You to Lay It All Aside,* revised and updated ed. (Lake Mary, FL: Charisma House, 2007).

32 "Making Space for God to Work" by Tricia Lott Williford, Proverbs 31 Ministries, August 25, 2021, https://proverbs31.org/read/devotions/full-post/2021/08/25/making-space-for-god-to-work.

33 Some content taken from *This Book Is for You: Loving God's Words in Your Actual Life* by Tricia Lott Williford. Copyright © 2021. Used by permission of NavPress, represented by Tyndale House Publishers, a Division of Tyndale House Ministries. All rights reserved.

34 Corrie ten Boom with John and Elizabeth Sherrill, *The Hiding Place* (New York: Bantam Books, 1974), 238.

35 Taken from: *When Your Past is Hurting Your Present*, Copyright © 2005 by Sue Augustine. Published by Harvest House Publishers, Eugene, Oregon 97408. www.harvesthousepublishers.com.

36 Kurt Kaiser, "Pass It On," from the musical *Tell It Like It Is* (Waco, TX: Lexicon Music, 1969).

37 James Strong, *Strong's Exhaustive Concordance of the Bible* (Abingdon Press, 1890).

38 "The Irony of Shalom" by Tim Mauricio, Weekly Devotional, Calvary Chapel Santee, accessed June 25, 2022, https://ccsantee.com/the-irony-of-shalom/.

39 "When Pain Prompts Us To Cry Out to God" by Kia Stephens, Proverbs 31 Ministries, November 16, 2021, https://proverbs31.org/read/devotions/full-post/2021/11/16/when-pain-prompts-us-to-cry-out-to-god.